Mohammad Aamir Khan was born in 1977. In 1998 he was kidnapped, tortured and framed in eighteen bomb blast cases. It took him fourteen years to prove his innocence and now he is a free man. When he finally came out of jail he was stepping out into a drastically changed world—his father was dead and his mother paralyzed. He had no job and no security. Despite the daily challenges to survive and support his family he has involved himself in the struggles of people fighting discrimination and oppression. Aamir has worked for NGOs involved in the area of democratic rights and secularism. His work in Shabnam Hashmi's Anhad took him to various corners of India and he has become a part of the community of activists fighting against discrimination in various spheres—religious minorities, prisoners' rights, the oppression of women and the rights of the LGBT community. Aamir has been widely interviewed by national and international media. He has used the opportunity to speak eloquently on issues relating to human rights and democracy and has emerged as a powerful voice of democratic India. Aamir is married to Alia, who waited fourteen years for him. They live in Old Delhi with their daughter.

Nandita Haksar is a human rights lawyer, campaigner, teacher and writer.

FRAMED AS A TERRORIST

My 14-year Struggle to Prove My Innocence

Mohammad Aamir Khan
with
Nandita Haksar

SPEAKING TIGER

SPEAKING TIGER PUBLISHING PVT. LTD
4381/4, Ansari Road, Daryaganj,
New Delhi–110002,
India

First published by Speaking Tiger in paperback 2016

ISBN: 978-93-85755-22-4
eISBN: 978-93-85755-23-1

10 9 8 7 6 5 4 3 2 1

Typeset in Sabon Roman by SÜRYA, New Delhi
Printed at Sanat Printers, Kundli

To the memory of Abbu Jaan and Ammi Jaan
and special thanks to sweet Alia

CONTENTS

THE CONTEXT

This is a story about Aamir, an ordinary young man born in a Muslim family living in the by-lanes of Old Delhi; a youth who dreamt of a conventional future for himself: marriage, family, a nice home and a decent job.

Aamir's dreams were cut short when he was kidnapped by the police and found himself accused of being a terrorist, planting bombs and being in league with dreaded Pakistan-based militants. And the bizarre events led to his imprisonment which lasted nearly fourteen years.

Aamir's story is exceptional because despite all he and his family suffered, he refused to give up the values and principles he had been brought up with. He sees his secular and democratic values as a bequest left to him by his father, a committed member of the Congress Party, even though the Congress Party itself had betrayed those values.

Aamir has been a witness, even while he was behind bars, to the rise of Hindu fascism and Muslim fundamentalism; he has seen the invisible walls rise up between the Hindu and Muslim communities. Despite this Aamir continues to build bridges between communities. At least a part of the reason for Aamir's belief in the values of secularism and democracy is found in the history of Old Delhi, where he was born and where he grew up and lives even now.

Growing Up in Delhi-6

Old Delhi was once known as Shahjehanabad; the city built by the Mughal Emperor Shahjehan in 1648. Shahjehanabad was a beautiful city with leafy trees and gardens and the beautiful fortress-palace called Qila-Mubarak which faced the stunning mosque, the Jama Masjid.

Even as late as the1780s there were sixty bazars in the city and plenty of food. Delhi survived the Afghan and Maratha invasions and then the British took over the city from the Marathas in 1803. Despite all these invasions Delhi was proud of its unique and vibrant culture which united Hindus and Muslims in a camaraderie rarely witnessed in other parts of the country.[1] The number of Hindus and Muslims were consistently equal and both could be seen at the court, the gatherings in Chandni Chowk, around the dastan-gos, at weddings and the annual Gul-faroshan, the festival of flower-sellers celebrated by both Hindus and Muslims, which has survived till today and is known as Phool Walon ki Sair .

The love of Urdu language, courtly etiquette, the weekly musha'ras, the patangbazi and the kabutarbazi—all were a part of a shared culture and civilization.

This unique culture was given a deathly blow in the aftermath of the revolt of 1857 when the British crushed India's first war of independence. The Red Fort and the Jama Masjid were occupied by the British troops; Muslims were banished from the city as also the Hindus who took part in the uprising.

Mirza Ghalib, Delhi's most famous poet, a witness to the decay and destruction of his beloved city lamented: '*Allah Allah Dilli Na Rahi, Chavni Hai, Na qila, na shaher, na bazar, na nahar; Qissa mukhtasar—shahar Sahra ho gaya...*' (Oh Allah! Delhi is no more; it is now a cantonment, no fort, no city, no bazars, no canal; in a word, the city is a desert).

Shahjehanabad had become Delhi and after 1912 it was called Old Delhi in contrast to the New Delhi which was being built by the British as their new Imperial capital. Sometimes Old Delhi is called the Walled City even now; an allusion to the time when the city was protected by thirteen gates. Today the Kashmere Gate stands as a silent reminder of the times gone by.

The British abolished the old chowkidari system and replaced it with a new police force which was heartily disliked by all, even the Europeans and loyalists. They employed Gujjars and Jats and promoted stereotypical images of Hindus and Muslims as two separate and antagonistic communities. A legacy which plagues us till this day.

Then came the violence and agonies of the Partition. British India was partitioned into two sovereign states, India and Pakistan. The Partition was perhaps the most cruel and bloody in history. Some two million Hindus, Muslims and Sikhs were murdered in the violence and seventeen million people were forcibly transferred between the two countries.[2]

By the time Aamir was born the transformation of Old Delhi into Delhi-6 was complete. It began with the influx of the Punjabi refugees and later migrant workers from all over India. From a beautiful city known for its gardens and canals, its bazars and its culture, Old Delhi is now a commercial slum known by its pin code: 110006 or, simply, as Delhi-6.

Old Delhi or Delhi-6 is the smallest district in terms of size with an area of 25 sq. km, and a population of 5.7 lakh according to the 2011 census; a population density of 23,149 persons per sq. km.

90 per cent of Delhi-6 is a slum with noxious and obnoxious factories housed in 616 katras, 260 kuchas, 193 kachchi bastis and 87 pakki bastis and 274 mixed ones with no proper ventilation, drainage or sewer lines besides being messed up with fatally dangerous electricity wires hanging overhead that cause recurrent fires.[3]

The Muslims of Old Delhi find themselves ghettoized within narrow by-lanes. Many have been impoverished since the time of the Partition and cannot afford education for their children or medical treatment for the elderly; they live in constant fear and uncertainty, victims of state and communal violence and now more recently of the so-called war against terror.

Aamir was born in Delhi-6. As he grew up the by-lanes of his neighbourhood were tense; the Muslims felt increasingly under siege. There was a growing Muslim resentment and anger against an attack on their religion; whether it was the Shah Bano case in 1985; the Rushdie affair in the 1990s and the demolition of the Babri Masjid in December of 1992. Aamir's father watched the rise of Hindu fascism and, as a reaction, the growth of radical Islam but he kept his son safe from physical violence and any influence of communal ideologies. Aamir grew up knowing that there were dangers lurking outside but he had no idea how terrifying they could be. His was a happy childhood.

An Amateur Spy

In many ways Aamir is a victim of Partition. His own family was partitioned when his older sister married a Pakistani. Thus for the families who were divided by international boundaries the Partition is not something which happened in the past; it continues to impact their lives on a daily basis.

Perhaps the most vulnerable victims of the Partition are those who are drawn into the dark and murky world of spooks, spies and sleuths. Both countries are involved in intelligence gathering and counter-intelligence in which the spies or couriers get caught and are subjected to brutal torture and imprisonment for long years.

The intelligence agencies do not take responsibility for their agents or their families. Many a family has lost their only breadwinner in this way. It is only recently that stories of these couriers and spies are coming out in the open. For instance, Ravinder Kaushik, a man who worked as a RAW agent in Pakistan from the time he was 23 years old was finally caught and died in a Pakistani jail. He is neither celebrated nor a hero for his country. Even though his family claimed that Bollywood film *Ek Tha Tiger* was based on his story the film's director denied it.

Aamir was recruited to be a courier, but not given any training. Published reports state that even couriers are given training; and the training capsules of four weeks entail learning the basics of intelligence activities—how to identify military vehicles, officers' ranks, and the art of covering their tracks.[4]

Aamir did not have the skills or training to be a courier, he had never smuggled anything even into his classroom let alone across the border. He was travelling under his own name and if he had been caught not only would he have landed in jail but his sister's family would have been suspected of being Indian spies. It would have most certainly ruined them.

And the strangest part of this shadowy world is that Aamir never knew the identity of the men who recruited him; or to which agency they belonged. Unlike most Western countries, in India the intelligence agencies do not have any clearly established and credible accountability mechanism. Therefore the agents, such as the shadowy Guptaji who contacted Aamir, are never made accountable for their actions. The intelligence agencies are not subject to public scrutiny and are exempt from the ambit of the Right to Information laws. They are not accountable to the Indian Parliament.

Aamir did not read spy stories and he had no ambition to become a hero. Therefore, he did what any untrained person would do when asked to smuggle something across a militarized border: abort. He ran to the safety of his home, his country.

Police Brutality

The human rights movement in India, and abroad, has focused the world's attention on the violence perpetuated by those who are charged with the duty of enforcing the law and keeping us safe from crime.

Late Justice Anand Narain Mulla of the Allahabad High Court famously observed: 'There is not a single lawless group in the whole of the country whose record of crime comes anywhere near the record of that single organised unit which is known as the Indian Police Force.'

Not only has the police force become more brutal since he wrote those much quoted words, they are given rewards and medals despite committing unspeakable crimes against hapless citizens.

Take the examples of officers of Delhi's Special Cell: Assistant Commissioner of Police, Rajbir Singh, was caught by the Central Bureau of Investigation (CBI) in a corruption case in 2005. It was alleged that he used his position to extort money from builders. Yet he was a recipient of many awards.[5]

In fact, three other officers involved in false encounter i.e. murder of citizens, received the President's Police Medal for gallantry in 2010.

In international human rights parlance these crimes are examples of extrajudicial acts by the police and other security forces. These include: extrajudicial arrests (Aamir rightly called it kidnapping), extrajudicial killings (false encounters or custodial deaths due to torture) and extrajudicial detentions or illegal imprisonment. None of these words conveys the full horror of the acts of vile brutality by the police.

The human rights community has, for long, called for reforms of the police.

The conversations about police reform are based on different concerns. One which has been highlighted more recently is that communalism has been institutionalized within the police force mainly because of a lack of recruitment from the Muslim communities. The remedy that is recommended is to have more Muslims in the police force.

This demand has most vociferously been articulated by the Muslim leaders. While the demand has some validity it does not go to the root of the problem.

It is important to remember that merely having more Muslims in the police force will not solve the problem just as having more women in the police force will not stop violence against women.

Efforts to recruit more members of minority ethnic groups or races into police forces in the United Kingdom and the United States has not led to the eradication of institutional racism.[6]

Among the most heinous crimes committed by the police is torture which is banned under international human rights law. Human rights groups in India have been documenting the institutionalized use of torture by both the police and the security forces, including the armed forces. These reports are publicized and a general public awareness has been created.

However, the issue of torture has not taken the centre stage in Indian politics as it has in the United States of America after the media exposed the brutality of torture methods used in the Abu Ghraib detention centre. American citizens have been shocked and outraged and sparked off a national debate on the use of torture against prisoners. In India there has been no moral outrage against institutionalized brutalities by law enforcement agencies.

On the contrary. Oftentimes the public in India has demanded that more powers be given to the police to arrest and detain, lowering the standards for fair trials, and harsher punishments for the convicted. These demands have the effect of lowering international human rights standards and this in turn has political consequences which could endanger the security of the country.

A highly trained interrogator of the US military, Chris Mackey, who has written a book called *The Interrogators*[7] has concluded:

> 'The reason the United States should not torture prisoners is not because it doesn't work. It is simply because it is wrong. It dehumanizes us, undermines our cause, and, over the long term, breeds more

> enemies of the United States than coercive interrogation methods will ever allow us to capture.'

Allowing our police to commit crimes with impunity and not making intelligence agents accountable has led to serious undermining of the protections guaranteed in our Constitution. The international human rights community has found another euphemism—Amnesty International calls the extrajudicial system 'the shadow system of justice'. To my mind the word 'justice' is entirely inappropriate.

While the human rights community has worked for the abolishment of torture and the death penalty and reform of the police, those who have actually been victims of police brutalities have argued forcefully that the police as an institution should be abolished. While doing research for this book I came across a blog which had posted '50 Reasons to Abolish the Cops!'[8] I showed it to Aamir. He laughed but asked: 'How can that be possible?'

The Insidious Art of Framing

Human rights lawyers stress the importance of pre-trial procedural safeguards for the protection of the accused; specially protection from torture in police custody and also to ensure a fair trial.

At the pre-trial stage the role of the magistrate

before whom the accused is produced is crucial; the magistrate can ascertain whether the accused has been tortured, whether the arrest has been made legally and whether the accused has been given access to a lawyer. The doctor who examines the accused at this stage can record whether the accused has been tortured.

Aamir was denied all these safeguards by the police, the magistrates and the doctors. These safeguards are routinely denied to almost all poor people who are arrested or kidnapped by the police. The denial of these rights helps the police to frame people in false cases by allowing them to elicit false confessions, fabricate evidence and instil fear in the accused so he does not speak out.

The police would find it very difficult to frame people if these procedures are followed in letter and spirit.[9] Therefore, it is important to understand step by step how Aamir was framed: Aamir was in effect kidnapped by the police in the night so there was no record or witnesses to his arrest; there was no record of the names of police officers responsible for the arrest or the circumstances of his arrest. This was in clear violation of the procedures laid down by law as well as the Supreme Court.

Since there was no record of the time of arrest, Aamir could be kept in illegal custody and the police could torture him and break his will to protect himself.

If he was arrested legally he would have to be produced before the magistrate within twenty-four hours. In this case he was kept for eight days at the police station without access to a lawyer, magistrate or any relative.

Aamir could have died in police custody and there would have been no record of his disappearance or his death. In human rights jargon this would have been an enforced disappearance. Official statistics show that on an average four people die every day in India in either police or judicial custody.[10]

This was the time the police was able to obtain Aamir's signatures on innumerable blank pieces of paper and make him write into blank diaries. And they made him give false confessions to people injured in the bomb blasts so that they would later identify him in court.

When the police finally produced Aamir before the magistrate, the magistrate did not bother to ask Aamir when and how he was arrested or whether he had access to legal advice. On the day Aamir was first produced in court the magistrate, the lawyer and the police spoke in English, a language Aamir did not understand.

The doctors, with the exception of one, too failed in their duty to uphold the ethics of their profession. They should have honestly recorded the injuries they found on Aamir—the trauma he was going through and other details of his torture.

The courts allowed the police to have remand for nineteen cases even though there was prima facie no evidence against Aamir except the so-called disclosure statement he was supposed to have made while he was in police custody. Every judge knows that a disclosure statement or a confession made to the police is not admissible in law.

Aamir was kept in legal remand for nearly two months in which time the police created further evidence in order to frame him in nineteen bomb blast cases. Aamir was made to sign blank papers, write in diaries, and give false statements that he had bought chemicals from shopkeepers to make the bombs.

Procedural safeguards are very inadequate protection against violation of human rights by the police; but enforcement of these procedures can often save a person from death in police custody, torture or from being framed.

The Supreme Court of India laid down guidelines for all arrests. These guidelines are now a part of the law of the land:

1. The police personnel carrying out the arrest and handling the interrogation of the arrestee should bear accurate, visible and clear identification and name tags with their designations. The

particulars of all such police personnel who handle interrogation of the arrestee must be recorded in a register

2. That the police officer carrying out the arrest shall prepare a memo of arrest at the time of arrest and such memo shall be attested by at least one witness, who may be either a member of the family of the arrestee or a respectable person of the locality from where the arrest is made. It shall also be countersigned by the arrestee and shall contain the time and date of arrest.
3. A person who has been arrested or detained and is being held in custody in a police station or interrogation centre or other lock-up, shall be entitled to have one friend or relative or other person known to him or having interest in his welfare being informed, as soon as practicable, that he has been arrested and is being detained at the particular place, unless the attesting witness of the memo of arrest is himself such a friend or a relative of the arrestee
4. The time, place of arrest and venue of custody of an arrestee must be notified by the police where the next friend or relative of the arrestee lives outside the district or town through the Legal Aid Organisation in the District and the police station of the area concerned telegraphically within a period of 8 to 12 hours after the arrest.

5. The person arrested must be made aware of his right to have someone informed of his arrest or detention as soon as he is put under arrest or is detained.
6. An entry must be made in the diary at the place of detention regarding the arrest of the person which shall also disclose the name of the next friend of the person who has been informed of the arrest and the names and particulars of the police officials in whose custody the arrestee is.
7. The arrestee should, where he so requests, be also examined at the time of his arrest and major and minor injuries, if any present on his/her body, must be recorded at that time. The 'Inspection Memo' must be signed both by the arrestee and the police officer effecting the arrest and its copy provided to the arrestee.
8. The arrestee should be subjected to medical examination every 48 hours during his detention in custody by a doctor on the panel of approved doctors appointed by Director, Health Services of the concerned State or Union Territory, Director, Health Services should prepare such a panel for all Tehsils and Districts as well.

(D.K. Basu versus State of Bengal (1997)
1 SCC 416.

Why did the police frame Aamir? One explanation could be that they were under enormous pressure to arrest someone in the Delhi blast cases. Or was it just greed? They knew they would get a large cash award. But why was Guptaji and the intelligence agencies a party to this massive frame-up? In India the intelligence agencies have been set up by executive orders and not through Acts passed by the parliament. Therefore there is no accountability to the people or the parliament.

There is no record of how many people have been framed by the police; how many have been able to prove that they have been framed and whether any policeman has been punished for framing an innocent citizen. While it is true there is a disproportionate number of Muslim youth who are being framed in false cases, the police frame people in other circumstances. For instance, Premlal was framed in eighteen false criminal cases from 1991 to 2007. It started when he reported a theft in his house and the police recovered the goods but did not return them. Premlal then filed a series of criminal cases and he spent seven years in jail. In 2010 he filed for Rs 60 lakh compensation but he was awarded only Rs 5.62 lakh. The police were not punished.

While it took the police two months to frame Aamir it took him more than fourteen years to prove his innocence.

Proving Innocence

The idea that a person is innocent till he or she is proved guilty is not a modern one. It has been a part of Islamic jurisprudence as well as Roman criminal law. It is based on a simple assumption that most people are not criminals therefore the burden of proof should be on the person who declares, not the one who denies.

Under Indian criminal law the accused is presumed innocent till the time the Prosecution can collect and present in a court of law compelling evidence of guilt. This presumption of innocence is the cornerstone of human rights jurisprudence. Even after spending nearly fourteen years in jail, being acquitted in seventeen cases and being released Aamir is still fighting to prove his innocence.

It seems that under the Indian criminal justice system it is easier to prove an innocent man guilty than for an innocent man to prove his innocence. The criminal system justice system works in many ways against the innocent, especially if they are poor and cannot afford competent but expensive lawyers.

The most crucial time for an accused is the time immediately after his arrest, especially an illegal arrest. I asked Aamir whether he had asked his mother what she had done when he did not return the day he was kidnapped. He said he never had an opportunity to find out what she did all those days when he did not return and his father was away. Even when her husband returned from Allahabad they were not at all sure what to do.

Aamir asked what she could have done. I said she should have reported to the police station or sent a telegram to the Indian Human Rights Commission. He looked at me incredulously. Did I think ordinary, honest folk know all these procedures?

Aamir said that in the beginning, each time when his mother visited him in the jail, she would just cry with tears rolling down her cheeks. It was only much later that she told him that a man called Mohammad had come and asked for his passport and identity papers. The man had produced a note written to her by Aamir in Urdu. That is why she handed him all the documents. How could she have had an inkling that the man was a police officer and her son's note was extracted from him after torture?

The defence lawyer should have asked the mother and tried to find out all that happened after her son disappeared. Her testimony would have proved that the police was telling a lie about the time and date of arrest. The police claimed to have arrested Aamir on February 28, 1998 when in fact they had kidnapped him eight days earlier on February 20, 1998. Her testimony could have proved that he had been illegally arrested and detained long before the date of arrest written in the First Information Report and the police story would have been disproved.

Aamir's mother was finally produced as a defence witness during his trial in Ghaziabad in 2011; that too on the suggestion of the trial court judge. By then her speech was slurred and she came in a wheelchair.

The remarkable aspect of Aamir's trials were the Prosecution witnesses. Many of them were victims of the bomb blasts and they could have succumbed to the pressure of the police to identify Aamir as the man who was responsible for the blasts. But these witnesses refused to believe the police and they refused to testify falsely.

The prosecution declared their own witnesses hostile and cross-examined them; normally it is the defence lawyer who should cross-examine the prosecution witness. Even under relentless cross-examination the witnesses refused to lie.

From 2000 Aamir was denied the right to be tried in an open court. His trials should have been held in Tis Hazari, which was nearer to his parents' home. But the court allowed the trials to be held in the court deep inside the Tihar Jail complex. Why did the court allow this and why did the defence lawyer not challenge the decision?

In case after case the judge acquitted Aamir. He

recorded in his judgements that the prosecution witnesses did not support the prosecution story and he acquitted Aamir . However, in several judgements the judge said he was acquitting Aamir by giving the benefit of doubt to him. There was no one to question the judge and ask him that if there was no evidence then where was the question of benefit of doubt. This fact would be used later to deny Aamir compensation for illegal arrest, torture and illegal detention for nearly fourteen years.

The war against terrorism had not even officially begun but the political atmosphere was already surcharged; the media celebrated the arrest of every person accused of terrorism but did not report when an innocent man was acquitted. A Muslim accused in a bomb blast case would inevitably be presumed guilty even before the trial began. Things would get much worse by the end of 2001.

Politics of Hatred

There are many extrajudicial factors that impact the outcome of a trial or whether a trial takes place at all. These are the media, the political atmosphere, prejudices of the judge and the attitudes of the public at large.

In India's war against terrorism the first casualty has been human rights standards. The anti-terrorism laws have invariably reversed the burden of proof. In other words, the accused is presumed guilty until he can prove himself innocent.

While in jail Aamir met many Sikhs and Muslims arrested under TADA, the Terrorist and Disruptive Activities (Prevention) Act, 1985. Although the Act had lapsed in 1995 the men who were arrested under that law were being tried under its provisions.

By that time the anti-terrorist law had been proved to be ineffective in curbing terrorism and had led to the arrest of hundreds of people in Gujarat, where there was neither any terrorist activity at the time nor was there any insurgency.

On 24 August 1994 Union Minister of State for Home, Rajesh Pilot, told the Parliament:

> 'Of the approximately 67,000 individuals detained since TADA came into force, 8,000 were tried and only 725 persons were convicted. Some 59,509 people had been detained with no case being brought against them. The TADA Review Committees found that except in 5,000 cases the application of TADA was wrong and asked for the withdrawal of cases. Despite the admissibility of the confessions made to the police as evidence—which were invariably made under torture—the conviction rate was less than 1 per cent. Yet, thousands of people underwent prolonged detention without ever being convicted. The maximum numbers of arrests under TADA were not

> made in Punjab, Jammu and Kashmir or Northeast India but in Gujarat, which had no record of terrorism. The majority of the victims belonged to religious minorities.'[11]

Aamir was himself treated as a terrorist from the time he entered the jail. The jail authorities wanted to put him in the high risk cell even though he was barely twenty years old and a first-time offender. When he was first sent to jail, the doctor refused to certify him fit to live in the isolation wards where even grown men with firmly held political beliefs went mad.

But Aamir was sent to the high-risk cell after barely two years of his detention and that is where he stayed for most of the time he was in prison. The cell was like a cage. He was deprived of his rights to study, to use the library or play games. He could go out of his small cell for just two or four hours a day and the rest of the time he was confined.

Putting a person in isolation inside a cell or a cage, even though he is an undertrial prisoner amounts to giving punishment even before conviction. This is often justified on the ground that the prisoner may try to escape or do harm to others.

It was during his detention in the high risk cell that Aamir met many political prisoners[12] mainly Sikhs fighting for Khalistan and Muslims dreaming of Caliphate.

Aamir noticed the growing number of Muslims in the high security cells. He was troubled by this fact and he tried to understand the reasons why. Aamir asked the men from SIMI for answers. SIMI, or the Students Islamic Movement of India, had been banned in 2001. [13]

A study of SIMI, established in 1977 and banned in 2001, concluded: "Given the pervasive social inequity of India's Muslim population, the internationalization of jihadi groups operating in the guise of social justice, and India's domestic barriers to developing a robust internal security apparatus, India's citizenry will remain vulnerable, as will other domestic and international terrorism targets within India."[14]

Aamir could easily have been attracted to the SIMI. He came from the kind of vulnerable background which could have led him to join SIMI. Aamir listened to these leaders, learned about the grievances of Sikhs, Kashmiris and also Muslims in general. He understands the historical reasons for many of the radical movements and is impressed by the integrity of many of the leaders. But he does not dream of a Khalistan or a Caliphate.

The most remarkable aspect of Aamir's struggle to preserve his integrity is his refusal to give up the secular and democratic values instilled in him by his parents.

Abolish the Prisons

There are nine million prisoners in the world. And the figure is growing.

Recent debates on the prison system have been focused largely on the rise of Muslim youth in prisons, both in the West and in India. Many of these youth have been framed in false terror cases. Increasingly, the states are justifying these frame-ups in the name of national security; and as a result international human rights standards have been significantly lowered by anti-terrorism laws.

The number of Muslim convicts in British prisons has surpassed the 11,000 mark for the first time, according to a new report 'Prison Population Statistics'. The statistics show that the number of Muslim inmates in England and Wales jumped to 11,248 in 2012, up from 3,681 in 1997. Stated another way, over the past fifteen years, the number of Muslims in British prisons has jumped by more than 200 per cent.[15]

The increase of Muslim inmates in British prisons is eight times faster than that of the overall prison population, and the numbers show a clear over-representation of Muslim convicts: Muslims, who make up roughly 5 per cent of the British population as a whole, now make up 13 per cent of the British prison population (compared to just 6 per cent in 1997).

In India there is a similar trend. The statistical data

of the National Crime Record Bureau (NCRB) from year 2001 to 2012 shows that the percentage of Muslims in prisons of the total prison population has been always greater than the share of Indian Muslims in the country's population.

The data also shows that nearly 55 per cent of the Muslim convicts are in the jails of four states—Maharashtra, Madhya Pradesh, Uttar Pradesh and West Bengal.

While it is of utmost political importance to highlight the fact that a disproportionate number of Muslims are in jail the fact remains that the largest number of people in the jails are the poor; this is true for Western jails as well as in India.

The prime targets of the unjust criminal justice system are the poor. And often the root cause of the Muslim anger is that the community has been deprived of its just and due share in the country's development. This is a fact that seems to have been pushed to the background in the current discourse on prisoners' rights.

In India, so many poor people are languishing in jail even after they have been acquitted only because the system and their family just forgot them; in 1983 the Supreme Court released Rudul Sah from the jail fourteen years after he was acquitted. In 2005 the National Human Rights Commission released

Machung Lalung from a jail in Assam after being in jail since 1951; he had already spent forty years in jail after completing his sentence. Vijay Kumari, a woman in Kanpur, who had been granted bail nineteen years ago, was finally released from jail in May 2013 after her son—born in a jail—grew up to earn enough money for her bond money.

It is true that even now, by global standards, India locks up a lesser number of people than many other countries. Some 370,000 inmates (two-thirds awaiting trial) are spread across nearly 1,400 jails. That represents approximately 30 persons in prison per 100,000 people, a far lower incarceration rate than in China (170), let alone America (730).[16]

US prison statistics show that nearly 50 per cent of the prisoners are black and 18 per cent are Hispanic. However, the curious fact is that despite these figures most prisons are located in white neighbourhoods.[17] While prisons are used as instruments for oppressing minorities they have another function which is barely visible in India so far.

Prisons are a source of livelihood for a growing number of people and corporations. It was found that in the USA a prison warden could make himself a millionaire if he owned a single pay phone. The US telecommunications corporation AT&T estimated that inmates of prisons across the country made long distance calls worth one billion dollars annually.

There are no comparable figures in India; but now it becomes clear why Tihar Jail has recently started allowing the prisoners to make calls. It also explains the rapid expansion of its economic activities such as a bakery and a restaurant; and recently a mobile factory has opened an ancillary unit in Tihar—an obvious source of cheap labour.

The Supreme Court has recently ordered the release of all undertrial prisoners who have spent half of the maximum sentence prescribed for the offences they are charged with. The court has assigned the task to lower judicial officers to visit each jail under their jurisdiction from 1 October 2014 and complete the task of releasing them within two months. However, there is no news of how far the task has progressed.

The Supreme Court order is just a step in the direction of prison reform. Many people have been calling for abolishing imprisonment as a form of punishment altogether.

There is an increasing awareness that the prison as an institution is obsolete. Joan Baez sang 'We shall raze the prisons to the ground' in the 1970s and Angela Davis, the American black leader, has said that the prison needs to be abolished as the dominant mode of addressing social problems that are better solved by other institutions.

It is no longer Quakers, anarchists and political

activists who are calling for the abolishment of prisons but the UN has also published a report 'Alternative to Imprisonment'[18] which observes: 'The overall use of imprisonment is rising throughout the world, while there is little evidence that its increasing use is improving public safety.'

Aamir's case is a dramatic example of why prisons should be abolished.

National Outrage

After hearing Aamir's story people all over India have expressed sympathy. All too often his case is upheld as an example of how justice ultimately prevails. The media has praised the lawyers who fought on his behalf, the judges who acquitted him and the NGOs who gave him employment. But no one has called for a radical reform of the criminal justice system.

There has been no moral outrage in our country. Police accountability and prison reform is not on the political agenda of any political party or even human rights organization. Bollywood continues to celebrate police brutalities and extrajudicial justice.

Although Aamir is no longer behind bars he is not truly free.

The fact remains that even now he is fighting to prove his innocence. He has been acquitted in seventeen cases. However, the trial court convicted him in three cases. He has filed appeals. He won his appeal when the Delhi High Court acquitted him in the case of the bomb blast in Karol Bagh in which he was given life imprisonment. That case was of 1997; the trial court gave its judgement in 2003 and in 2006 the Delhi High Court acquitted him stating: 'Prosecution failed to adduce any evidence to connect accused appellant with charges framed much less prove them. Judgement of conviction set aside.'[19]

However, two more appeals are pending before the Delhi High Court. Even though Aamir has already served the sentence for crimes he did not commit he wants the courts to set aside the false convictions. In a fourth case, he was made to pay a fine of Rs 5000 even when the judge observed that the Enforcement Directorate could not prove their case.

The fact remains that despite all the sympathy and support that Mohammad Aamir Khan has garnered he does not earn enough to be able to support his small family adequately; to plan a decent future for his child and to dare dream of a safe and secure future for himself.

The law in India does not have any rules to assess damages to people who suffer false imprisonment. The Innocence Project in the USA which provides pro bono legal and investigative services to individuals seeking to prove their innocence has come up with guidelines which are relevant for Aamir's case as well as for others who have been framed and falsely imprisoned. They are:

1. Access to immediate and ongoing financial assistance for all basic needs.
2. Access to free medical, dental, mental health and psychiatric care, including free medical insurance such as Medicaid.
3. Housing.
4. Assistance with any and all areas of community and family reunification/reentry, including educational and vocational training and assistance.
5. Access to professional client-centered case management by a professional trained in and sensitive to the issues related to wrongful incarceration and these entitlements.
6. Prompt and effective record expungement, with the accompanying transfer to the exoneree of all medical and other records maintained by the department of corrections that would be helpful to the exoneree in making the transition and acquiring continuing care.
7. A formal, official apology from the State or other relevant entity regarding the wrongful incarceration.
8. Access to free legal assistance for legal issues

that arose from the wrongful incarceration, including, but not limited to, back child support payments and student loans.

9. Monetary compensation at least at the established U.S. federal standard, which is currently $50,000.00 per year of wrongful incarceration regardless of any prior or future convictions.

(innocencenetwork.org)

In addition, the police officers and the intelligence officers responsible for framing him should be persecuted and punished. It is not only the police—the jail authorities are also liable to pay damages to Aamir.

The jail authorities should give compensation to Aamir for:

1. Violence against him inside the jail, the beatings, and illegal punishment such as keeping him in a high-risk cell and putting him in solitary confinement.
2. Not sending his papers to the other states to ensure he got speedy trials.
3. Organizing the attack on his life inside the jail.
4. Depriving him of his right to study at IGNOU, depriving him of the right to play games and see films.

5. Displaying communal prejudice and hatred.
6. Denying him adequate medical treatment

The magistrates and judges too played their part in prolonging Aamir's agony.

1. None of the magistrates ever asked him when he had been arrested; whether he had been tortured and how to ensure his safety.
2. The magistrates did not ensure Aamir was represented by a lawyer of his choice.
3. Judges wrote that he was being acquitted on grounds of 'reasonable doubt' when there was no doubt at all.
4. By delaying the trials.
5. For allowing the trials to be held inside the court complex thus denying him the right to trial in an open court.

There is no precedence in which jails and judges have paid compensation for the wrong they have done. Police are seldom punished for their wrongs.

This is the story of just one innocent victim of a vicious system. There is an army of wronged Muslim youth and non-Muslim poor who are perishing in jails without any hope of getting justice from an unjust and cruel system.

The only hope is: national outrage.

A Word of Thanks

The three people I wish to thank have one thing in common with me—we are all Delhiwalas with an undying faith that people of all communities can live together with dignity and self-respect: N.D. Pancholi for introducing me to Aamir, Shabnam Hashmi for agreeing to give Aamir time so he could come to me and tell his story and most of all to Aamir, for his trust and his love.

Nandita Haksar
New Delhi

NOTES

1. Description of Old Delhi is taken from Narayani Gupta, 'Delhi Between Two Empires 1803–1931' in the *Delhi Omnibus*, New Delhi: Oxford University Press, 2002.
2. There are no exact figures for the deaths or the migrations even among the various scholars who have studied the Partition of 1947.
3. Feroze Bakht, 'Dying Old Delhi' http://www.milligazette.com/Archives/.
4. Chander Suta Dogra, 'Flies on the Wall' in *Outlook*, 12 September 2005.
5. Abhinandan Mishra, 'The Curious Case of Delhi's Controversial Special Cell', *Sunday Guardian*, 30 March 2013, www.sunday-guardian.com/investigation.
6. Praveen Swami, 'Bias and the Police' in *Frontline*, vol.

23 issue 24, 2–15 December 2006, http://www.frontline.in/static/html/fl2324/stories/20061215002503300.htm.

7. Chris Mackey and Greg Miller, *The Interrogators: Task Force 500 and America's Secret War Against Al Qaeda*, New York: Back Bay Books, 2005.
8. '50 Reasons to Abolish the Cops!', http://abolishthecops.wordpress.com/2011/02/11/55-really-good-reasons-to-abolish-the-cops/.
9. Article 22 of the Indian Constitution states: No person who is arrested shall be detained in custody without being informed, as soon as may be, of the grounds for such arrest nor shall be denied the right to consult, and be defended by, a legal practitioner of his choice. Every person arrested must be produced before a magistrate within 24 hours of arrest. No person shall be detained without the authority of a magistrate.
10. The Bureau of Justice now keeps the statistics under its Deaths in Custody Reporting programme.
11. V. Venkatesan, 'Short on Strategy', *Frontline*, vol. 25 issue 25, 6–19 December 2008, http://www.frontline.in/static/html/fl2525/stories.
12. Except in West Bengal, the Indian jails do not recognize the category of political prisoner. A political prisoner is a person who has been imprisoned because of his political beliefs. Some activists have said all prisoners are victims of the system so are by definition political prisoners.
13. Yoginder Sikand, 'The SIMI Story', http://www.

countercurrents.org/comm-sikand150706.htm. By then the organization had some 400 full-time workers or Ansars and 20,000 sypmathizers or Ikhwans, in addition to a cell for young children aged between 7 and 11, called the Shahin Force. It also established a special wing to work among madrasa students and 'ulama, the Tahrik Tulaba-i Arabia.

14. C. Christine Fair, 'Students Islamic Movement of India and the Indian Mujahideen: An Assessment', The National Bureau of Asian Research, Washington http://ASIAPOLICY.ORG.
15. http://www.gatestoneinstitute.org/3913/uk-muslim-prison-population.
16. 'Tihar Prison in India: More Dovecote than Jail', *The Economist*, 12 May 2012, www.economist.com.
17. Joseph T. Hallinan, *Going Up the River: Travels in a Prison Nation*, New York: Random House, 2003 p. xviii.
18. UN Office on Drugs and Crime, *Handbook of Basic Principles and Promising Practices on Alternatives to Imprisonment*, New York: United Nations, 2007.
19. Mohd Amir Khan [sic] versus State 138 (2007) *Delhi Law Times* 759 (DB) (See Appendix I).

ABBU'S LAST WORDS

July 2001

The last time I met Abbu was in July 2001 at the Bara Hindu Rao Hospital. He was lying on the hospital bed. I knew he would not survive. That is why I had been brought there to have a last meeting. Abbu's eyes were filled with indescribable sadness but when he looked at me I could feel the warmth of his infinite love.

We looked deep into each other's eyes, conversing with words unspoken. It must have been so painful for him to see me, his son, his youngest child, standing in handcuffs, surrounded by uniformed policemen. Under those circumstances what could we have said to each other?

Abbu was not afraid of dying. It was living which had become hell. His son was accused of planting twenty bombs in trains, buses, bazaars of Delhi, Sonepat, Rohtak and Ghaziabad. My father knew in his heart that I had been framed; he knew his son could never be a traitor to his country.

Abbu's faith had been vindicated; the courts had already acquitted me in eleven cases. But I had been framed in nineteen cases; it could take many more years before I finally walked out of jail.

My father must have been tortured by the fact that after he passed away the burden of following the cases would fall on Ammi. She stood looking at both of us silently, with tears flowing down her plump cheeks. I could not even kiss her. I should have been the one to offer her comfort.

Abbu and Ammi watched as the police dragged me away. And then I heard Abbu's voice: '*Beta, main tumhari tareek par nahi aa saka.*' Those were the last words he spoke to me.

He was apologizing for not being able to be present in court for the trial. He had never missed a single date. My parents' lives revolved around courts, jails and visits to lawyer's chambers.

When I finally came out of jail after nearly fourteen years I found among his papers small chits with dates—the endless dates for court hearings. Ammi had carefully kept all the chits among his papers in a trunk.

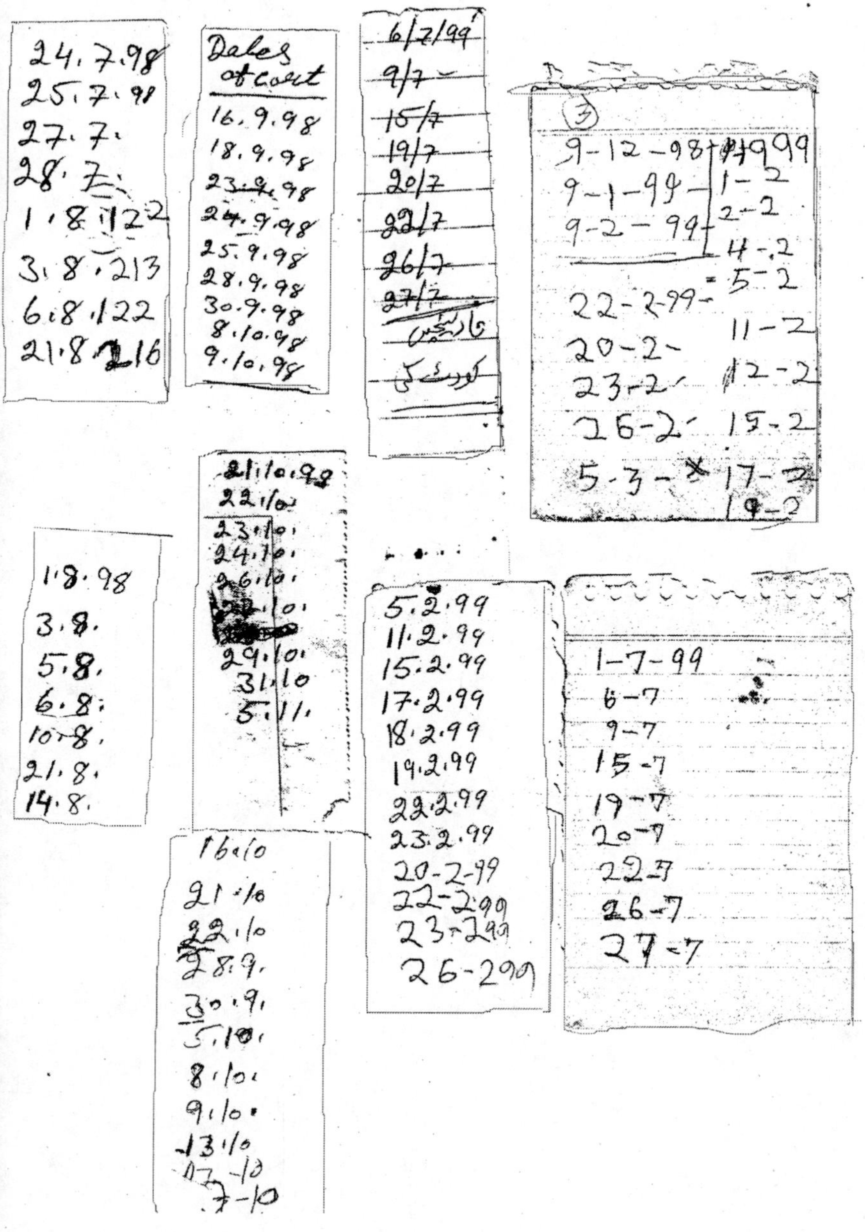

The chits with the dates of the Court hearings

1

GROWING UP IN DELHI-6

~

'I longed to visit Aapa, my sister Chaman Ara, in Karachi. I wanted to see Aapa and meet her family. I was also excited about visiting another country. For me Pakistan was as foreign a country as Germany except that in Pakistan they spoke the same language as us.'

I was born in my maternal grandmother's home. Nani, as I called her, lived in Mohalla Kishangunj, Azad Market, Delhi–6.[1] The midwife was a Christian nun who had been there when my eldest sister was born. I still regret that there is no photograph of the midwife who brought me into this world. After all, she is the first person who held me. My official date of birth written in my passport is 17 January 1977. But I am not sure whether that was indeed the day I was born because on other certificates there are other dates.

By the time I was born, Nana, my mother's father, was no more. He had died a few years before I was born. I wish I had met him because I am told he was a man of great dignity and loved by the people. My Nana's name was Maulana Abdul Latif Saheb. He worked as a Munshi in the Sadar Bazar Post Office. After office hours he would help people write letters to their relatives. In those days most people did not know how to read and write. However, if people asked him to write a lie or convey a falsehood, he would refuse to write it for them.

Nana belonged to the Rajput community[2] but because he had such a distinguished reputation, the Qaum-e-Punjabian community[3] respected him and invited him to live in their neighbourhood in which many educated people like principals of schools lived.

When Nana died he was buried in the Shidipura cemetery meant exclusively for that community.[4] It was because of Nana's connections that both my sisters were married into this community.

To reach my Nani's home, I had to go through a massive gate with spikes at the entrance. The gate was closed every night at ten after the Isha namaaz and opened early in the morning in time for the Fajr namaaz.

I have vivid memories of Nani's house because my happiest days were spent there. It was a two-room house on the first floor and had a big verandah. The verandah was partly covered but I could see pigeons flying in the open skies. I spent many happy hours of my childhood flying kites from Nani's roof.

My father's name was Mohammad Hashim Khan. He was a Pathan.[5] He came to Delhi from his village near Allahabad where he and his family owned land. He often went to visit his village and would occasionally take me with him.

Once when my father, Abbu, took me to Allahabad, we went to visit a relative who lived right near Nehru's house. Abbu showed Anand Bhavan to me with great enthusiasm and I remember being impressed by the sheer size of the house.

Dadi, my paternal grandmother, lived in the village but Dada, my grandfather, had died by the time I was born. My father's family had originally come from Afghanistan and had made India their home. However, at the time of Partition more than 30 per cent of my father's family had left for Pakistan[6] but my father chose to stay in the land of his birth.

Abbu and his brother moved from their village and settled in Delhi. He bought a small flat in the Kucha Pandit neighbourhood, near Sitaram Bazar which was about a seven-minute bicycle ride from Nani's house. We lived on the first floor in one big room, a toilet and a kitchen. There was a big terrace where we could sit and it gave us a sense of space. There was no gate to our gali and it was a mixed neighbourhood with several Hindu families living amongst us. I did not have much contact with them or have an opportunity to go to any Hindu homes.

Abbu did not have a fair complexion like his sister who looks like a pukka Afghani. He was of medium build with a long face and a small beard. When I was very young, I remember him wearing pants and shirts but as he grew older he wore kurta- pyjama, a waistcoat and a 'V.P. Singh topi' on his head. What I remember most about him is his smile. It was so warm and straight from his heart; his whole face would light up. But he was a proper Pathan and was quick to get angry. For instance, if someone was late for an appointment he would be furious. But I do not remember even one occasion on which he raised his voice when talking to me. He was never angry with me. I was his beloved. He loved sweets and bought something for me every day even though Ammi warned him that my teeth would rot if I was given so many sweets.

Abbu was a pukka Congress supporter. Every morning he would go out to the bazar to buy something for our breakfast and there he would have a cup of tea and meet his friends and fellow supporters of the Congress Party. They would discuss politics. Sometimes, when I accompanied him, I would listen to their discussions but I was never interested in politics.

Ammi's name is Miamuna Bi; she is barely five feet tall and was quite plump at one time. She has a round face with a very serene temperament inherited from her father. She has a fair complexion and was much more religious than my father. After all, she was the daughter of a Maulana. She knew Urdu, Persian and a bit of Arabic. Ammi loved reading Urdu novels. Abbu regularly bought her the Urdu digests such as *Pakeeza Achanchal* and *Shama* which serialized these romantic novels.

Ammi used to keep hens and potted plants on our terrace. She grew all kinds of flowers in the flower pots like roses, chameli and jasmine. Girls from our neighbourhood would come to our home and ask Ammi for flowers.

Ammi had a hen whom she called Cookie. This hen had a habit of flying off and across to neighbouring roofs from where she would call out for Ammi. I used to play with Cookie, chasing her. I also remember buying chicks and fish from Fatehpuri bazar to keep as pets. But invariably they did not survive and then I would cry my eyes out.

Abbu thought pigeon-flying as a sport was a waste of time so I never learnt the art of training pigeons but I took to kite-flying very seriously. Even when I grew up I found time to fly kites, especially on holidays.

I remember my mother scolding me often for going off to fly my kites and not coming back for meals. If she caught me running across rooftops or standing dangerously on the ledge, she would shout out asking me to return. She scolded me for flying kites in the hot sun. When I did not pay heed to her warnings she burnt my kites and charkha. Then I learnt to hide my treasure in my friends' homes.

I was so obsessed with my kite-flying that Abbu decided to get me a summer job during my vacations at a wholesale dealer of shoes. The shop was in Ballimaran[7]—and there I sat, dreaming of my kites.

The only other time I remember getting a scolding from any family member was from my eldest sister, Chaman Ara. One day, when I was very small and she was giving me a bath I called her 'kutiya'. I am sure I had no idea of the connotation other than it referred to a female dog. But my sister was furious and asked where I had learnt such dirty language. She burnt a matchstick and blew it out and while it was still hot burnt my lips to punish me for using foul language.

Other than these incidents I was never really scolded because I was an obedient son and did not disobey my parents.

The first school I went to was the one run by Mr and Mrs Prakash who lived below us on the ground floor. They ran the school from their home. Mr Prakash was a Hindu and his wife, whom we called Aunty, was from a Sikh family. They had three children, two sons and one daughter. The older son was brought up as a Hindu while the younger son, Punoo, grew his hair and was brought up to be a Sikh. The daughter, Achal, was the youngest and we called her Baby. I grew up playing with these children.

The school was supposed to be a good one in the area and the fees were quite high. I passed my third standard from this school. After this I was shifted to a government school.

Abbu and his brother Qasim Khan owned a factory at Anand Parbat. I have a vague memory of my father taking me on his bicycle to the factory and I remember there were huge machines which made labels for clothes. I remember being awed by the size of the gigantic wooden machines which made a lot of noise.

After I came out of jail, I found many of Abbu's papers which had been carefully packed inside a small tin trunk by my mother. There I found a flyer with a black-and-white drawing of the machine described as 'High Class Machinery', which could make: 'Woven Labels, Tapes and Laces.'

The other side of the flyer gave details of the work under the heading: 'Nature of Works'. It said: 'This machine enclosed herewith actually works for the manufacture of various varieties of labels for Hosiery, Tailoring, Spot and ready-made garments, frails, bells, sarees' borders etc with signs in any language and pictures of any person and things in any desired measurements.'

I remember Abbu telling me that new smaller machines imported from Korea were available now for the same job.

There was a dispute between my uncle and Abbu and they went their separate ways. My uncle took the factory and my father had to take a job in another factory in Roshanara Road as a supervisor.

My uncle made a claim to my father's share of the land in his village in Pratapgarh district. Even though my mother told my father to let it go my father filed a suit against his brother and the case went on for years. My father would go to Allahabad to attend the court sessions but he never discussed these matters with me and I continued to have good relations with my cousins.

I think it was because of the loss of business that my father took me out of the Prakashs' school and put me into Mazharul Islam Secondary School. It was a government school, not a madrasa. But I could study only for four years, passing my seventh standard, after which my father took me out of school so I could help him with his business. However, my parents kept a tutor who would come and teach me. I remember my teacher's name was Shabana and she always asked Ammi's permission to pluck flowers from her pots.

The strain and tension of the court case against his brother must have taken a toll on Abbu. He developed high blood pressure and he found it difficult to cycle to the factory. Then he had an accident in which he broke his hand. He had the accident in April 1990 but could not return to work for more than six months. In any case, the factory was shifted out of the Sadar Bazar area to the outskirts of Delhi.

It was because of these circumstances that Abbu decided to start a private business in toys. He bought the toys from manufacturers and sold them to wholesalers. These were all cheap plastic rattles, parrots, small cars, water pistols and squirt guns or pichkaris used during Holi to squirt coloured water. I started helping him in this business and so I could not continue my studies.

I had a few friends who also lived in the same

neighbourhood and we would meet at a tea shop and exchange news. But I would return home well before dark. In the evenings our family would sometimes watch television but before we got a TV my father heard the news on his prized radio. We would also watch soap operas from Pakistan. They were freely available in the bazar.

My eldest sister, Chaman Ara, studied in Aligarh but I do not remember what she studied. I just remember her always sitting with books. She was married to a businessman from Karachi called Mohammad Nasir Batla. He ran a business of carpets and tiles. He was from the Qaum-e-Punjabian community.

I do not remember much about her wedding except that when her palanquin was lifted, I cried and cried and ran after her crying 'Aapa Jaan, Aapa Jaan don't go.' Someone lifted me up and I looked into her doli and then I was put down. She went away with her husband to live in Karachi in Pakistan.

I call my other sister Aapi. Her name is Roshan Ara. I have only two memories of her wedding. The first was that I had so many cups of coffee that our family friend Zaki Bari noticed. He called me and warned me that if I kept drinking coffee I would be urinating all night. The second thing I remember is the journey to Agra for my sister's walima. I remember that some dacoits attacked us but we reached safely. Aapi's husband was also a businessman from the Qaum-e-Punjabian community and he lived in Bangalore so Aapi, too, went away.

After my sisters left home I was the only child with my parents. Ammi missed her daughters very much. She went to meet Aapa Jaan in Karachi several times. In those days many relatives and neighbours went to visit their loved ones in Pakistan; it was quite a normal part of life in Old Delhi. Abbu refused to accompany Ammi because he said he did not want to go to a country where Muslims killed each other. He said this often but he would accompany Ammi to the Pakistan High Commission and help her fill the visa form.

Sometimes I, too, accompanied Ammi and then I saw the long lines of people standing waiting for their visas; often in the hot sun without any provision for drinking water. Those who came from outside Delhi slept on the pavement or went to the Nehru Park across the road.

Ammi would return with all kinds of gifts from Karachi. There were toffees for me and clothes for herself and Abbu. I especially remember the Shahi Supari or betel nuts full of fragrance and covered in silver. But the most exciting thing that she brought from Pakistan were the video cassettes of Pakistani dramas and serials. The ones I loved the most were by a comedian called Umar Sharif.[8] I remember watching his *Bakra Qistoon Par* (Goat on Instalments) and how we all laughed.

We would rent a video cassette player to watch these Pakistani dramas but later Abbu bought a VCR, so our neighbours would come and watch shows in our home. Mrs Prakash would borrow the cassettes from us.

I longed to visit Aapa, my sister Chaman Ara, in Karachi. I wanted to see Aapa and meet her family. I was also excited about visiting another country. For me Pakistan was as foreign a country as Germany, except that in Pakistan they spoke the same language as us. But my parents said they would send me only when I was old enough to travel by myself. However, I did accompany Ammi to Bangalore to visit Aapi, my second sister.

I remember the first time we went there. Abbu, as usual, refused to go; he was not interested in seeing new places or in travelling. If he ever went out of Delhi, it was to visit his beloved village.

Ammi and I enjoyed going out—seeing new places and, of course, visiting relatives, especially our own family. The journey to Bangalore by train was a long one. As we went deeper south I noticed the people spoke different languages, which we could not understand. I also noticed that as we entered Karnataka the colour of the soil changed to rusty red. I was amazed to see the colour but no one could tell me why this was so.

My sister's home was near the cantonment in Shivaji Nagar. She lived in her home with her husband and five children. Her husband had a big wholesale shop at Chickpet which sold shoes and slippers. He used to get the leather goods from Delhi and Agra. He would take me to his shop and I sat watching the people all day, sorely missing my kites.

My brother-in-law took me on his Bullet bike to see Hindi movies, which he loved. He also took the whole family out sightseeing. I remember being impressed by the shops on Brigade Road and the beautiful Vidhan Sabha building. Bangalore was so green and wandering through the Lal Bagh was a treat for us because we never saw trees or even green lawns in the crowded bazars of Old Delhi. I loved the huge clock made with flowers. It was here that I saw a church for the first time but I don't remember the name. I noticed that the woman who came to clean our house wore fresh flowers in her well-oiled hair.

I was also deeply impressed with the way the people stood in queues without pushing and shoving as they did in Delhi at bus stops and elsewhere. In Bangalore people were so much more polite.

Ammi was thrilled with Russel market. We had

never seen a covered market and the vegetables, fruits and flowers looked so fresh. I loved the black grapes, which I ate to my heart's content while I was in my sister's home. I wished that we could have taken some back for Abbu but the grapes would not have survived the long train journey to Delhi.

But we did take back the delicious 'Chaubey-ki-Naan' from Bangalore. My nephew had brought this special roti which was filled with coconut. We liked it so much that whenever we visited Bangalore we bought lots of it to take back for all our neighbours and relatives.

I went to Bangalore several times. On one occasion we went to Mysore by video coach and saw the stunning Vrindavan Gardens. I also noticed the number of shops selling alcohol.

My sister served us typical South Indian breakfasts of dosa, idli and sambhar. Ammi loved to drink tender coconut water. On one occasion, my sister took me to a wedding so I could taste the food. The food was so different from ours. There I tasted a biryani with lots of dry fruits and dried prunes served with a sour dal tempered with rye seeds.

I remember the days before I was kidnapped and locked up behind bars as tension-free, except for our constant worry over Abbu's health. The fact that I did not have money did not bother me. I never got any pocket money except an occasional chavani or quarter of a rupee (twenty-five paise) and if I got one rupee it was a huge bonus. On Eid if I got Rs 50 it was like hitting a jackpot. I used to save money to buy kites and charkhis or sweets such as gajjar ka halwa or gulab jamun. The rest of the money I would give to Ammi.

Ammi and Abbu were always telling me to be home before dark. There were some days I remember I was not allowed to go out at all. Abbu said there was some trouble in the city and it was safer if we stayed indoors. I remember he mentioned words such as 'curfew' 'riots' and 'police firing'. But these words had no bearing on our lives, except that we stayed at home.

I do have scattered memories about incidents which made me aware that the world outside my home was not always safe and there was danger lurking in an undefined place.

One day I was on the roof with my kites when I saw the Shishganj Gurudwara burn. I could see the flames.[9] My friend Punoo cut his hair but I did not understand the significance of this act. It was during this time that Punoo's brother refused to go to the gurudwara and went only to the temple. I also remember the Sikhs shutting their shops and many ran into our locality for protection. And Abbu's friend Uncle Kuku came to stay with us for a few days.

I also remember a neighbourhood uncle who wanted to become a pilot. He was somewhat of a local hero because no one else had ever achieved something so big in our neighbourhood. He lived next door and had taken his training but had not yet given his exams. On the day he was to leave to give his exams there was a curfew[10] and despite his showing his identity card and exam admit card the police did not let him go. As a result, he never became a pilot. Now he sells knick-knacks on the pavement in Chandni Chowk or at the Sunday bazar. I remember this story because Ammi told me his story and even now I see him in our neighbourhood.

I was not interested in politics but I do remember Abbu always warned us to beware of the Sanghis who wore khaki shorts and black topis. He said they were dangerous because they hated Muslims. I had no idea of the difference between RSS, BJP and Jan Sanghi. For us they were all Sanghis. And we would see them early in the morning when they gathered, especially near the Town Hall.

We were also scared of the police because during Hindu–Muslim, tension the police took the side of Hindus and beat up Muslims. At least that is what I would hear from Abbu and sometimes from the bazar when I met my friends. I was told a distant relative of Ammi was killed by the police while he was trying to close the gate into his gali during the Hindu–Muslim riots in 1983 or perhaps it was in 1986. His brother, Mohammad Ahmed, whom I call Mamu, is still alive and he used to work for *Qaumi Awaz*. Now he is more religious.[11]

There was one time when Abbu came back home quite agitated. He told us that a young Muslim man had been shot dead by the police while trying to stop the rioting. His name was Subhanullah. Later, a chowk near Hamdard Dawa Khana in Lal Kuan was called Shahid Chowk to commemorate him.[12]

There is one thing I remember which did leave a deep impression on my mind. One day I noticed that a young man I knew, called Babbal, was hiding inside the lathe machine workshop that belonged to one Gulzar who lived in the next gali. I saw people taking food for him inside the shop and then locking him inside. I was curious and asked Praveen Baji, who lived near our home, what the meaning of this was. She told me that there was tension between Hindus and Muslims and the police were looking for young Muslim men. She said Muslim youth had to be careful. When she saw the fear in my eyes she said I need not worry—I was too small and the police would not take me away.

I remember Abbu remarking that the Hindus living in our neighbourhoods had started leaving Old Delhi and going to Shalimar Gardens, Rohini and Pitampura. The Prakash family also left but I did not understand why they were leaving.

Looking back, I do remember how Abbu's eyes sometimes had a troubled expression. After I came back home from jail and looked at his papers, I began to understand his concerns.

I found a letter from K. Rais Ahmad, the Chairman of the Minority Cell of District Congress Committee (I) Delhi City, inviting Abbu for a meeting at the office at Kucha Pandit to discuss a Minority Convention to be held on 7 June 1988. There is a delegate's badge with Abbu's name for the All-India Congress Committee (AICC) (I) National Convention Against Communalism held in 1990 and a letter of invitation from the Samaj Ekta Committee for a reception of the newly appointed DIG, Shujauddin Sajid Khawar, on Sunday 16 September 1990 at Hotel Ranjit. It must have been a big thing for a Muslim to be promoted to the rank of a high official of the police.[13]

From this memorabilia I assume Abbu was concerned about the growing communal atmosphere in the country and especially in our neighbourhood. I can understand why he used to caution us to stay at home and not wander around.

I found some photographs in the tin trunk. There is one of Abbu with some other men holding a 'pankha'.

It looks like it was made during the Phool Walon Ki Sair. But I do not remember Abbu ever mentioning the festival or taking me to attend it. I even found a photograph of my father in a newspaper. It was a photograph of a peace committee. I wish I had asked Abbu about his experience in the Congress Party but by the time these questions rose in my mind it was too late. Abbu had passed away.

Later, in 1993, after the Babri Masjid was demolished, I remember I saw young men wearing black armbands and going around in Old Delhi. But in our family Abbu would insist we stay at home and keep away from any trouble. I remember there were times when there was a curfew, we stayed cooped up in our home, but I never felt any threat to myself. I always felt that as long Abbu and Ammi were there I would be safe and secure.

And then there was Alia. She lived in the Azad Market area and was distantly related to us. The first time she came to visit us was with her father. She was studying in an English medium school which was co-educational. And as if that was not enough to shock people in the neighbourhood her school uniform was a dress, not a salwar-kameez and dupatta. All this was a cause of societal disapproval but her father was determined to give the best education to his daughter.

Perhaps because my parents were not judgemental,

her father sent her to our house during her summer vacations to learn cooking, sewing and Urdu from Ammi. I wonder what recipes Ammi gave Alia because she did not part with her culinary secrets easily. Even my sisters do not know the secret of how Ammi made shahi tukra and the masalas for her korma.

Abbu sometimes helped Ammi in the kitchen. He could make roti, rice and kali dal. I sometimes did some housework when I was with them.

I have no idea what Ammi taught Alia. I was just mesmerized by Alia's eyes. Her round face was full of innocence and she looked like Rishi Kapoor's wife.[14] In the beginning we would look at each other only when we thought that the other was not looking. If our eyes met we would turn away in utter embarrassment.

Alia would bring her mark sheets to show Ammi and she made sure I was listening to her speak of her achievements. On a rare occasion when I visited her in her home, she showed me trophies and cups she had won. She showed me a photograph of herself which had been published in the local newspaper in connection with some academic achievement. I was so captivated by her eyes that I cannot recall what she won those trophies for.

When we did finally begin to talk to each other, we discovered we had similar views and also our temperaments were very alike. But we never went out together or expressed our love for each other; not even once did we hold hands. Ours was a love which was undeclared, like in the old Hindi movies.

In 1993, Abbu and Ammi decided to sell our Kucha Pandit home because it was deep inside a gali and getting transport was difficult. Autos would not go inside and we would have to walk quite a distance. Perhaps they felt the need to move to a neighbourhood where they would feel safer.

For some time we lived in rented houses and then Abbu found a flat on the third floor in Anarwali Gali in Kishan Gunj. We had two rooms and a terrace. I think they preferred this area because it was where Ammi's relatives lived. I was happy because it was nearer Alia's home.

Even though there was tension in the city because of the unrest, I had wonderful dreams at night about a future where Alia would always be by my side. I did not have even the smallest premonition that such terrible events were about to happen that we would be separated for fourteen long years. I had no idea that the trip I was planning to Karachi to visit my beloved Aapa Jaan would be the cause of this terrible pain.

NOTES

1. Shahjehanabad had become Dehli and distorted to Delhi by the 1860s and after 1912 it was called Old Delhi. The pin code for the area is: 110006 hence it is now known as Delhi 6.
2. Many Rajput families converted to Islam.
3. Qaum-e-Punjabian/Muslim Punjabi Saudagar has existed in Delhi for 300 years. It is an urban-based, highly exclusive community of businessmen with no socio-cultural links with other communities. It is the most important Muslim merchant community of North India. Some embraced Islam a thousand years ago. Today they number less than 4000 according to a community census. K.S. Singh, *People of India*, Volume XX Delhi, New Delhi: Manohar Anthropological Survey of India, 1996, pp. 574–77.
4. This is the only known example of a separate cemetery for Punjabi Muslims in any Indian town. Narayani Gupta, 'Delhi Between Two Empires 1803–1931' p. 191 in *The Delhi Omnibus*, New Delhi: Oxford University Press, 2002.
5. Pathans are of Afghan origin and rank last in the Muslim caste system. K.S. Singh, 'Sayyids, Shaikh, Mughals and then Pathan', pp. 548–51, op cit.
6. Approximately 3.29 lakh Muslims moved out of Delhi at the time of Partition; and nearly 5 lakh non-Muslims entered Delhi. V.N. Datta, 'Panjabi Refugees and the Urban Development of Greater Delhi', p. 296 in *The Delhi Omnibus*, op cit.

7. Ballimaran has many shops for shoes and opticals. In one of the narrow alleyways in Ballimaran lived the great Urdu poet, Mirza Ghalib (1797–1869) who has left us a vivid account of the events of 1857.
8. Umar Sharif is a Pakistani stand-up comedian, and stage, film and television actor, writer, director and producer. Before the production of *Bakra Qistoon Par*, stage shows in Pakistan used to be in sophisticated poetic language. After *Bakra Qistoon Par*, stage shows became vibrant, funny and gritty. Johnny Lever called him a 'comic genius'. Umar Sharif was invited as a judge in the Indian comedy show, *The Great Indian Laughter Challenge*.
9. This must have been during the three days, 1 November to 3 November 1984 when there was large scale violence against Sikhs in Delhi (and other parts of India) following the assassination of the Prime Minister, Indira Gandhi, on 31 October 1984. She was shot dead by one of her own bodyguards who was a Sikh. In the violence that followed (organized by members of the Congress Party) more than 2000 Sikhs were killed and their property destroyed.
10. There was a series of curfews imposed in Delhi after riots between Hindus and Muslims. The riots in 1986 and 1987 resulted in a number of deaths.
11. *Quami Awaz* was an Urdu daily founded by Jawaharlal Nehru in 1938 to uphold the values of secularism. It was closed down in 2008.
12. Aamir is referring to the police firing in Old Delhi on

14 February 1986. The crowd of more than a 100,000 namazees were returning after the prayers at the Jama Masjid. Muslim volunteers were present at each gate to ensure there was no untoward incident. Two young men, Mohammad Zakir, aged eighteen and Subhanullah, aged twenty-one (mentioned by Aamir) entered Gali Qasim Jan where there was no tension. The police fired on them and they died. See *Terror in the Walled City: An Investigation into Police Firing on February 14 and Subsequent Developments*, New Delhi: PUCL, March 1986.

13. The Sachar Committee's findings (2006) showed that the under-representation of Muslims in police forces across the country has contributed to institutional communalism and a persistent failure to defend the community's basic human rights.
14. Rishi Kapoor is a Bollywood actor and his wife is Neetu Singh.

2

AN AMATEUR SPY

~

'If I got caught I would land in a Pakistani jail and the thought made me shit scared and I returned back to the safety of my sister's home. I realized I did not have the stuff of which spies are made. In fact I have never been interested in stories of spies and detectives.'

By the time I was nearing twenty years of age, Abbu and Ammi decided it would be all right for me to visit Aapa Jaan in Karachi. I was old enough to look after myself. I was quite excited as I set off to get my visa. I was particularly interested in seeing the big foreign cars which zoomed about on the streets of Lahore and Karachi.

Although for me the idea of going to Pakistan was an exciting one it was not at all something out of the ordinary for the people in our neighbourhood. Neighbours, relatives and friends regularly went across the border to visit their near and dear ones. In earlier days, talk about Pakistan was a part of normal conversation in our neighbourhood. Nowadays no one dares talk about having relatives in Pakistan.

It was for this reason I did not mention that my older brother Yahya Khan was also in Pakistan apart from my eldest sister. He had gone there around the time of Chaman Ara's wedding. He married there and settled down there. Abbu and Ammi were very hurt because they had thought he would be the one who would look after them in their old age. They were so angry with him that they cut him off and he was never mentioned in our home. I hardly remember his face and Aapa Jaan did not even mention him when she phoned from Karachi. I had only very vague memories of him and now I have no idea where he is or what he is doing. For our family, he might as well be dead.

I applied for a visa four or five months ahead of the time I intended to go. It takes very long for the Pakistan High Commission to issue a visa and they ask all the details of the persons to be visited and the reasons for visiting. I filled up all the details and asked for a visa only for Karachi although I would have loved to visit Lahore. They used to give separate visas for each place to be visited.

It was a bright day in November when I set off to get my passport and visa from the Pakistan High Commission. I was lost in thought as I tried to imagine what Karachi would be like. I was really excited. I got my travel documents without any problem and was walking towards the bus stop to return home when I was accosted by a man who introduced himself as Gupta from the Intelligence Department.[1] I did not ask to see his identity card. The thought did not even occur to me.

Guptaji asked me to walk with him to a kiosk near the Teen Murti Nehru Planetarium where he offered me a cold drink. He asked the particulars of my visa and then asked whether I was willing to do something for my country. He said he would provide full security for my family and I would be paid for my services. Without knowing what I was committing myself to, I answered I was willing to serve my country. He took down my address and promised to contact me in a few days.

A few days later, Guptaji came to my house. This time he was accompanied by another man who was taller and addressed Guptaji as 'Sir'. We walked to a kiosk selling cold drinks at the Azad Market crossing where he explained my task. He said I was to take photographs of the Naval Headquarters at Shah Faisal Road in Karachi; he wanted me to take photos of the vehicles used, the signboards and some other details.

The man accompanying Guptaji told me that I should take the decision to do this work without any pressure and assured me that if I completed the task I would be given full security, protection and financial support. He then took down details about me and my sister's address and telephone number in Karachi.

On 12 December 1997, I was at the Old Delhi railway station ready to catch the Samjhauta Express[2] when once again Guptaji appeared. This time he gave me a camera, his pager number (this was the time before mobile phones were widely used) and Rs 5,000. Guptaji also told me that one Mr Choudhury would contact me and give me some documents which I must bring back to Delhi.

I guess I was very naïve and had no idea what I had let myself into. But at that moment I was excited at the prospect of meeting Aapa and Bhai Saheb, seeing a new place and enjoying a good holiday. There was a big crowd at the station. I think there were more people to see off their relatives than there were passengers. People had huge amounts of luggage.

Many went to Pakistan for business purposes. For instance, some were carrying helmets which cost around Rs 500 each in India but in Pakistan they fetch Rs 5,000. Paan is very expensive there so people take betel leaves to sell there. I was carrying a basket of paan leaves for my brother-in-law in a small basket. Apart from that I also had presents for my sister and my nieces and nephews.

It was around nine at night when the train left the station and we reached Attari early in the morning. It was cold and misty and the tea shops had not yet opened. We kept sitting in the train which was warmer. When the sun came out we got out of the train and sat on the benches. The platform was very clean.

At around ten in the morning the Customs people arrived and we began to form a queue. Those who had a large amount of luggage called the coolies but I could handle my own luggage and did not want to waste money on a coolie. The Customs people checked my luggage and stamped my passport. Now I had to wait for all the passengers to be checked and it was evening by the time our train came. I was very tired, thinking that the bus would have been much easier. We got into the train and it started off. I heard the sound of horses' hooves and saw the Border Security

Force (BSF) men riding alongside our train. We were approaching the international border. I began to feel a strange excitement but was also a little tense. I was thinking: What will it all be like?

I guess everyone was feeling the same because they were all craning their necks and looking out of the train window. The doors of the compartments were sealed so no one could hang out of the doors. There must have been at least four people at each window. I, too, looked out and saw the watchtowers from where the BSF guards trained their guns.

We passed green fields fenced off with rolls of barbed wire and openings where there were gates painted black. At the border the train stopped, our soldiers checked all around and then a black gate opened. I felt a strange disquiet mixed with sadness as we left India, the way one does when one leaves home.

We entered Pakistan and now it was their Rangers who accompanied us. There was a big signboard in Urdu welcoming us to Pakistan. We had arrived at the Wagah railway station.[3] The signboards were in Urdu, the coolies wore different coloured uniforms, and the Rangers carried different kinds of arms. The coolies spoke in Punjabi. And I felt I had entered a different world within a short distance. Now I was in a strange country with a passport. The passengers with heavy luggage took trolleys and I heard someone call out that Indian and Pakistani passport holders should form two different queues. I remembered Ammi telling us that over the years the procedures and checking had become more strict and complicated. She also said that Urdu-speaking people were not treated well in Pakistan.[4]

My luggage was searched and then I bought the ticket for the Karachi train. I could not go out and explore because my visa was for only one city so I wandered around the platform and peeped into the waiting room, which was full of people. There was no room for me there so I sat on a bench and waited till the evening for my train to Karachi.

In a way things were familiar because people wore the same kind of dress and the food was also familiar. I saw samosas, jalebis and fruits being sold. But I was surprised that everyone spoke Punjabi instead of Urdu.

It was late in the evening by the time my train to Karachi arrived. I knew that the journey would take some 20-22 hours so I tried to settle myself in. I found the train was not as comfortable as our trains especially the small cushion protruding out of the backrest which I found uncomfortable.

In the morning, I sat by the window and watched fields, the trees and the houses go by. They looked familiar. The chaiwala who sold tea called out in the same way as he did in our trains. But now I saw the men wearing kameez-shalwar instead of kurta-pyjama. By the afternoon I noticed the language had changed and everyone was speaking Sindhi. The attire was the same but the men were wearing Sindhi topis. Then we passed a sandy stretch and I realized that I was seeing a desert. On the platforms there were vendors selling non-vegetarian dishes such as korma, roti and biryani—something which is rare at home in India.

We reached Karachi in the night. I got down on the platform and at once saw my sister and brother-in-law at a distance. Aapi had put on weight and had become quite stout. She looked much older than what I remembered. It felt strange meeting her after so long and she hugged me tight and cried. Bhai Saheb picked up the luggage and when we went out I thought we would be getting a taxi. But they had their own Toyota and it was wonderful to travel in my sister's own car.

It was a 20–25 minutes' drive and even though it was night the market was abuzz with activity and the shops were lit up. I was thrilled to see such broad roads and imported cars, like the type I had never seen before. There was heavy traffic and the buildings were so much bigger than the ones I had seen in Old Delhi.[5] It was all such a contrast to the narrow lanes and tangle of electricity wires I was used to.

My sister lived in a big three-bedroom flat on the first floor of a six- or seven-storey building. The moment we entered I noticed a big white swing in the drawing room. They even had air conditioners in their home. I admired the tiles and the beautiful furniture and then I noticed that the walls did not have paint but wallpaper with exquisite roses. My brother-in-law had a wholesale business in wallpaper.

I had barely time to take in all the beauty and elegance of my sister's flat because I was surrounded by her seven children, all calling me Mama. They wanted to know what I had brought for them from India. Their faces were full of expectation and I really enjoyed playing with my nieces and nephews. Even though I was tired I felt revived and my sister soon had dinner ready. She said she had got a Karachi special for me. It was called 'khatakhat', a dish made with liver and kidney. It was delicious.[6]

But I could not eat as much as I would have liked to because I was so tired and overwhelmed by all the emotions: the tension of the journey and the happiness of meeting my sister and her family. I would have liked to sleep but the children were waiting to see what I had brought from India. I had paan and attar for Bhai Saheb; special aam papar and sweets for the kids; mehendi and chikan-work kurtas for my sister and coconuts for everybody.

Of course, the highlight of my trip to Karachi was when I first set my eyes on the sea. I remember Bhai

Saheb parked the car and we walked towards the water; and it stretched on and on as far as the eye could see. And the movement of the waves fascinated me as we walked towards the water. We took off our slippers and walked on the sand. Then the sand became wet and I became aware of the roaring of the sea and felt scared. When the first wave came and splashed at my feet, I gasped. It was fun but very scary and I held on to my sister's hand on one side and my niece's hand on the other because I was afraid I would be swept away as the sand under my feet seemed to slip away.

But little by little I conquered my fear and walked deeper and deeper into the sea till I was knee-deep, but still holding fast onto my sister's hand. The kids really loved being on the beach and it turned out to be a wonderful day at the beach.

I saw ships anchored far away and I longed to go for a ride in the sea. Bhai Saheb fulfilled my wish when he hired a boat for the whole day. Our whole family got into the boat. I was told my sister did not usually go for these boat rides because she was too scared since the boat rocked and no one ever thought of wearing life jackets.

We went past big ships and I was reminded of the scenes from the film *Coolie*. Amitabh Bachchan goes to the dock from where pilgrims go for the Haj in a big ship and there is loud honking from the ship before it sets sail. My sister pointed out that the ships going east were going to India while those going in the other direction were going to Saudi Arabia.

From the boat I saw colourful buoys bobbing up and down and my brother-in-law explained what these were. We were all given small fishing rods while the boatmen had long fishing rods. They caught fish and it was fried on our boat. I had never tasted such fresh fish before.

During the weekdays I would accompany Bhai Saheb to his shop and I loved to look at the bazars and on the way saw the Teen Talwar monument. I was very surprised to see many streets, mohallas and big buildings still had Hindu names. I do not quite know why but I felt good seeing this.

On weekends my sister and brother-in-law would take me out somewhere or the other. We would go to the beaches or to Manora Island. On one occasion we went to Clifton Park which was like the Appu Ghar in Delhi where Abbu took me. But here there were many different kinds of rides. The one I liked most was the cars whirling around like jalebis in hot oil. I also saw video games for the first time in my life.

Before the month was over I fell sick. My sister took me to the doctor and I was diagnosed with jaundice so I had to rest at home. This gave my sister and me time to chat. She wanted news about everyone, she asked about each family member and the neighbours and then I could see how she missed the friends and family she had left behind. But I also saw the contrast between our lifestyles—the problems of living in the narrow lanes of Old Delhi and the luxuries she and her family enjoyed in Karachi.

My brother-in-law told me he was a supporter of MQM.[7] I did not really understand politics but I was surprised to learn of the discrimination against Urdu-speaking people in Pakistan.

Apart from jaundice I also had pain in my stomach. A few months before coming to Karachi I had experienced the same acute pain. I went to the doctor. I was asked to get a coloured X-ray and prescribed some medicines. But Abbu and Ammi used to have herbal medicines and said Western medicines had too many side effects. So I had got some Unani medicines.

Bhai Saheb took me to a famous hakim in Karachi. He said I had stones in the kidney and prescribed a medicine called Neer. He also told me about a shop near my home in Delhi where I would get it once I reached India.

I had begun to feel better when I got a call on my sister's landline. It was Guptaji, reminding me of the work I had promised to do. One day I made some excuse and took the camera and went on my own to Shah Faisal Stadium and walked towards the Naval

Headquarters. When I saw the security arrangements there, I was terrified. If I got caught I would land in a Pakistani jail and the thought made me shit scared. I then returned to the safety of my sister's home.

I realized I did not have the stuff of which spies are made. In fact, I have never been interested in stories of spies and detectives. But since I had promised Guptaji, I did try one more time to see if I could find some safe place from where I could take photos and not be seen. But this time I was again too scared to take out the camera. All this time I had hidden the camera at home in case my nieces and nephews demanded that I take photos of our picnics. It was not a digital camera. It had a roll so I could not have separated the personal pictures.

I had been given one other task, which seemed a little easier. I was to meet a man by the name of Choudhury at Sabir Hotel. I went to the hotel on 5 February. Mr Choudhury easily recognized me and quickly gave me a small leather bag; if I remember correctly, it was yellow in colour. I took it and hid it in my bag.

I did not breathe a word of these activities to my family because I knew they could get into trouble. It was time for me to return and on 11 February 1998 I left Karachi by train and arrived at Lahore the next day. I carried back gifts for Ammi and Abbu apart from the presents sent by my sister and Bhai Saheb.

I saw other Indians going to Lahore. I, too, longed to go and see the Badshahi Mosque and roam around the fabled Anarkali market but I was too scared. I bought the ticket for the train ride to Wagah. Then I stood in the line for the security search before we were allowed to get into the Samjhauta Express. I carefully watched the searching and I was really shocked to see the authorities taking out everything from the passengers' bags and suitcases. The searching was very thorough. There was no way I could have hidden the leather bag. And if they opened it, I was done for.

I broke out in a sweat. I imagined myself in a Pakistani jail. Then I remembered my promise to Guptaji. But there was no way I could see of getting past Customs and my fear of being caught was rising. I panicked. I went to the back of the queue and then I saw the toilets at the other end of the platform. I walked fast to the toilets and took out the leather bag. With all my strength, I threw it onto the top of the roof of the toilets. I heard the thud as the bag fell and I looked to see if anyone had seen me or heard the noise. No one seemed to have noticed. My heart was still thumping when I joined the line of passengers.

My turn came, my luggage was searched and my passport stamped. I noticed the Customs people and the others were not very friendly. I sat in the train. My heart was still beating fast when I got into the train and waited for it to start. By afternoon the train started crawling out of the station but before we reached the border, it suddenly stopped. My heart was in my mouth. I thought they had stopped the train because someone had found out about me.

When we crossed the border and reached Attari, a distance of three kilometres, I sighed with relief. Then I looked around and noticed many men and women who had come from Pakistan were dressed very differently. The women had designer burkhas and they all looked much better dressed. They seemed to be travelling together for some special occasion. I asked one of them and she told me that they were Qadiyanis who were going to visit the birthplace of their founder in Punjab, on the Indian side of the border.

On 13 February 1998, I reached home and the safety of the arms of my beloved Ammi and Abbu. Abbu was planning another trip to Allahabad but had waited for me to come back. I distributed the presents among the relatives and neighbours. I gave Ammi the masalas I had brought from Karachi. My sister had insisted they were better in Karachi; and khus khus is cheaper there. Burkhas and chadors are also better there—Alia tells me that the quality of cloth is the same but the designs and colours in Pakistan are so much brighter. From India the presents that relatives in Pakistan look forward to are chikan work from Lucknow, artificial jewellery made in Sadar Bazar and paan. Anyway, I don't really remember the details of the presents I had brought but I distributed them. I slept because I was tired, partly by the long journey but mostly by the tension.

Abbu left for his village the next day.

NOTES

1. Aamir never found out the real name of this Guptaji or the name of the intelligence agency to which he belonged. The officer could have been from the Intelligence Bureau or from India's external intelligence agency, the Research and Analysis Wing (RAW) or some other. The intelligence agencies are outside the ambit of the Right to Information Act and there is no mechanism for making these agencies accountable to the law or courts.
2. Samjhauta, a word common to both Hindi and Urdu, means agreement/accord/compromise. The train connects Amritsar in India to Lahore in Pakistan which is a distance of 42 kilometres. The train was for a long time the only train link between the two countries and it was started in 1976 as a result of the Simla Agreement signed in 1971.

   Following disturbances in Punjab in the late 1980s, due to security reasons Indian Railways decided to terminate the service at Attari, where customs and immigration clearances take place. On 14 April 2000, in an agreement between India and Pakistan, the distance was revised to cover just under three kilometres—Attari to Wagah.

3. Wagah is 22 kilometres from Lahore and three kilometres from Attari.
4. Urdu-speaking people in Pakistan are called Muhajirs and form the majority in Karachi. But they have been subjected to discrimination and have been victims of communal violence.
5. Aamir had till that point never really been around New Delhi with its tree-lined avenues and broad roads.
6. Khatakhat is originally from Karachi in Sind, but is now very popular throughout Pakistan. It is made from offal (that is, a mixture of various meat organs), including brain, kidney, heart, lamb chop and testicles in butter. The dish's name is an onomatopoeia from the sound of the two sharp blades that hit the griddle as they cut up the meat.
7. Muttahida Qaumi Movement, generally known as MQM, is a secular political party founded in 1978 mainly representing the Urdu-speaking population. In 1997, the MQM officially removed the term Muhajir (which denotes the party's roots among Pakistan's Urdu-speaking citizens) from its name, and replaced it with *Muttahida* ('United').

3

HOW I WAS DENIED EXTRAJUDICIAL JUSTICE

~

'I stubbornly refused to sign the papers. They brought some instruments and started pulling out the nail of my toe. I screamed but did not sign. My tormentors threatened to pull out the nails one by one till I signed all the papers. I could still hear the screams from the other room. I did not want to think what they were doing to the man. I signed and signed and signed.'

The day after I arrived back home from Karachi, on Saturday 14 February 1998, I messaged Guptaji on the pager number I had been given to inform him that I was back in Delhi. I was keen to return his camera to him. He asked me to meet him at a kiosk in Azad Market. It was a quarter of a mile from my home under a tree. The kiosk is no longer there.

I returned the camera and told him why I could not do the work and accomplish the mission he had assigned to me. I told him there was just too much security. I had expected he would be disappointed and upset but I had not anticipated how angry he would be. He accused me of harming national interest and said I had thrown away a chance of helping my country. He then told me he would give me two more days to find the documents.

I wondered how he could expect me to produce those documents when I had already told him that I had thrown them away. On 17 February I met Guptaji again. This time it was in a restaurant. I knew he would be angry because I had not been able to find his bag, but how could I produce it when I had thrown it on top of the toilet roof in Wagah?

But this time Guptaji was not just angry, he also threatened me with dire consequences if I did not find those papers given by Choudhury. He accused me of being a Pakistani agent. He said I must have been recruited by the Pakistani intelligence services. I repeated my story and he said so many Indians had managed far more difficult tasks and I could not smuggle one small bag. He refused to understand how scared I had been.

This time his tone had an edge to it. He said I had no idea what he could do to me. He warned that if I did not do as he said he would ruin my life. Guptaji called me a liar and I kept pleading that I was innocent. On earlier meetings I realized he was angry but I thought he was justified in being angry since I had failed to carry out the tasks given to me. But now I began to feel threatened. Fear was creeping into the marrow of my bones.

When I returned home, I wondered what I should do to convince Guptaji that I was telling the truth. After all, it was not as if I had been given any training at all. How could I smuggle a bag with secret documents past the watchful eyes of the Pakistani authorities?

A few days later, on Friday, 20 February, I told Ammi I was going for the night namaaz and that from the mosque I intended to go to the medicine shop to buy the medicine prescribed by the Hakim Sahib in Karachi. Ammi was cooking in the kitchen and Abbu was still in his village. I went for namaaz and then started walking towards Bahadurgarh Road in Sadar Bazar towards the medicine shop.

The wholesale market had closed. They closed much sooner than the retail shops and, as I walked, there were not many people around. It was dark and the winter chill was still in the air. From the corner of my eye I saw a white Gypsy vehicle ahead of me. As I advanced, it started moving very slowly and I instinctively walked faster.

Suddenly I was pushed violently from the back and I fell. Some people came out of the Gypsy and caught me before I fell and pulled me into the car. I was pushed down onto the floor of the car. My hands were quickly tied and I was blindfolded.

Although I was very scared, I managed to ask why they were kidnapping me. I thought they were criminals who were looking for someone who would help them get ransom money. It could not be any enmity because Abbu had no enemies as far as I knew. I really thought the people who had pushed me into the vehicle were criminals. I had no idea that the police could break the law and indulge in kidnapping. That is why I picked up the courage and asked them what they hoped to get from me. One man replied that I would soon know what they would get.

After about half an hour, the vehicle stopped and I was taken down. I was made to walk. I could sense that there were several people there. I could hear another car. I heard someone say 'come behind us' and that 'the work is done'. The tone and tenor of the voice was like that of Delhi's Jat bus conductors and drivers. This convinced me even more that I was in the hands of criminals.

I stumbled into a drain and got hurt. I was lifted out. After that I could feel I had been brought into a room. Here they took off my blindfold and untied my hands. I saw ten to twelve men standing facing me. They looked strong and muscular and dehumanized. No one said anything, except one who ordered me to take off my clothes. I was so embarrassed. They had no shame. They made me take off all my clothes and when they saw I had no underwear, one man remarked: '*Saale yeh underwear bhi nahi pahente.*'(Bastards, they do not even wear underwear). I presume by 'they' he was referring to Muslims.

Then all of them started hitting me. I was slapped, kicked, elbowed, boxed and my hair pulled so hard that I thought my neck would break. All the while they also abused me verbally. I had never heard such dirty and violent language. The abusive language was full of anti-Muslim innuendos. The only word that comes to my mind which describes those men is 'jallaad'.[1]

The men seemed genuinely angry and their anger

had destroyed their humanity and ability to feel any compassion for a fellow human being. They kept beating me till I fell down and blood came out of my mouth. I felt numb except for the excruciating pain in my broken right jaw.

I kept asking them why they were beating me and screaming 'Hai Ammi, hai Allah' till I fell unconscious. But the torture had just begun.

When I came to, I found I had been propped up against the wall which had white tiles. Some other men were sitting on stools and chairs. They spoke in a better tone and started asking me questions. I was in no position to ask who they were and why I was being interrogated.

They asked me my father's name and address and about my family. If I took time to reply I was abused and slapped by my persecutors. Then I noticed Guptaji was present in the room. I cannot say what time it was but it must have been late at night. He sat on the chair and he used really violent and abusive language. He demanded that I tell the truth. He said I still had time so I should tell the truth. He again asked about the bag with the papers I had been given in Pakistan. He asked me whether I had given the bag to someone else. I repeated my story and I was beaten again. Guptaji then said to the musclemen standing by:

'*Isko garam karo. Abhi yeh seedha nahi hua.*' (Warm him up. He has not been straightened out).

Some of the men left. By now I realized these were policemen. There were around five or six left to carry on their heinous work on my body. They made me sit up straight against the wall. One caught my right arm and the other my left arm so I was immobilized. Then one caught my left leg and the other my right leg. One of them held my stomach down.

I watched in absolute horror as the two men slowly and deliberately started pulling my legs apart till they touched the back of the wall. I screamed. I cried out for mercy. At least I was able to scream and cry. That was my only freedom. The muscles in my legs were literally torn apart and I lost sensation in them. Then they brought my legs back together. I again fell unconscious. When I recovered consciousness, the torturers lifted me up but I could not stand. They released me and I fell with a thud. Two or three times I was lifted up and allowed to fall. Now there was no way I could escape.

Guptaji was sitting there throughout. The policemen kept urging me: '*Bolo jo Saheb kaheten hain woh batao*.' (Speak and tell Saheb what he wants to know.)

Next they dragged me to a dark part of the room. My hands were tied at the back and I was lifted up with a chain. All my weight was on my shoulders. In seconds the pain was unbearable. I felt the muscles of my arms break. I felt I was dying. They were standing and watching as if it was a spectacle. I lost consciousness again.

When I came to I found myself on the floor, my body racked in pain and I was unable to move my arms. My mouth was dry and I wanted a drink of water. They refused to give me even a sip of water. I noticed Guptaji was still in the room.

The torturers dragged me to a bench and made me lie on it. One really bulky man with red hair, a moustache and a face which seemed incapable of ever smiling, sat on my thighs. My head was hanging down. Another man caught my hair and held my head down tight. Someone held down my hands and my legs.

The guy who was sitting on me held a pipe from which water gushed with high pressure and he kept it pointed on to my nostrils so I could not breathe. If I tried to breathe from my mouth then they would put water into my mouth. I was allowed to breathe for barely a second before they switched on the water. I felt as if my brain was filled with water.

Then they propped me up and made me drink water from a jug. They gave me so much water that my stomach was swollen and a man jumped on my stomach till water came out of my mouth.

I saw light come into the room. It was morning. I was no longer thinking of home or my parents or anything else. All I could feel or think was pain. I had no control over my body; I urinated and defecated there. They gave me a little rest but it was only because they were getting ready for the next round of torture. It occurred to me that the torture was like a routine. No one told anyone what to do. They had it all planned. From the next room I heard screams of pain. I felt like sleeping but I was not allowed to sleep. They said they had also been awake all night so I could not sleep. I was shivering with cold and sneezing.

Guptaji asked me who was there in my home. I said only my mother because my father was away in his village. He told me to write a letter to my mother stating that I had to go away on urgent work and that I would return soon. They also asked me to tell my mother to hand over my passport and identity cards to the bearer of the letter. I tried to resist with whatever strength I had but it was of little use. I had been broken and had become their slave.

Guptaji went away but my tormentors were ready with the next phase of their torture.

A man stood with rollers on my thighs and rolled it up and down like they do for road construction. I felt my muscles were becoming like mincemeat. They did this two or three times and then made me lie on my back. They pressed the rollers from the back of my thighs to my back. I could hear the bones breaking. I was screaming. I could not turn or move or lift myself.

My legs were numb and I lay crumpled on the cold cement floor. My head felt so heavy. A man came in carrying a stethoscope so I presumed he was a doctor. He checked my blood pressure. After that I was given a cup of tea and a few stale slices of bread. The tea was watery. I was in the habit of having milk but now tea tasted like nectar. I was propped up against the wall. I could not even hold the cup. Perhaps they put some medicine into the tea because I felt some relief from the pain.

I lost all sense of time. The torture continued on and on. I was allowed to sleep just enough to recover for the next session. The blankets were very rough and stinking with bedbugs crawling all over them.

They kept asking me about the papers and on one occasion Guptaji said because of me one of their agents had got caught. I could not understand what he was saying. My body was numb. I asked for water. They gave me water mixed with detergent and made me drink it. My stomach was filled with gas and felt very uncomfortable.

Just when I thought I had been through it all, they brought battery and electric wires. They put the wires around my fingers and on my nipples. The battery was operated by hand. I do not know how many volts I was administered but the jolts made me unconscious.

I do not remember on which day but one morning

the 'nice guys' came back. They said it was stupid of me to put up with so much pain. I should just tell them what I had done with the papers. I said I was innocent. I repeated my story.

This time the 'nice guys' sat around a table eating samosas and gulab jamuns and sipping tea and coffee. The smell of the food awakened my appetite and I felt so hungry. I was longing to have something to eat but I did not ask them and they did not offer me anything.

I felt I was dying. I said I was dying but they assured me: '*Tujhe marne nahin degey*.' (We won't let you die.) It was more of a threat than a consolation. They were keeping me alive only so that they could continue to torture me. They gave me roti and watery dal. But I could not open my mouth because my jaw seemed to have become dislocated. They threatened to force-feed me so I managed somehow to eat something.

One morning they blindfolded me and took me outside. They had to support me. I could feel that I was walking on grass. I was made to hug a tree. Then they pulled my arms around it and the bark was very rough. Then they started to hit me on the back and I screamed. I became unconscious. They hit me on the back of my legs and buttocks and spine and then took me back to the room and removed the blindfold.

I was back in the room. I could hear the cries of pain of someone else being tortured next door. The police now started playing cards while I lay naked in the corner. In between someone came and slapped me and the verbal abuse never stopped.

They tortured me in shifts, normally at night. They would wake me up from my sleep by shining a flashlight on my face—then make me stand up and keep me standing for hours. If I was about to fall, they would let me sit down.

It seemed that they tortured me just for the pleasure of seeing me in pain or humiliating me. They poked me with a needle, urinated on me and on one occasion they put my hand under a chair and sat on it. Between the chair and my hand there was something with a spike. It hurt like mad. They put petrol into my rectum. It made me scream. While interrogating me they would routinely slap me and once Subhash Tandon[2] even burnt me with his cigarette butt. He was one officer whose name I cannot forget because I saw him later in court. I had got to know the names of several of my tormentors.

By the fourth or fifth day the torture was less. I am not counting the occasional slap, the kick or verbal abuse. They started to give me medicines one or two times a day so the pain was less.

One day I was blindfolded. I could walk with support and was made to climb up the stairs. The blindfolds were removed and I saw I was in a lovely room with an air conditioner. There was a desk and officers were sitting around. Guptaji was also present. There were some new faces I had not seen before.

Again I was asked the same questions. They asked me what all I had done in Karachi. I told them what I had done and how I had seen the tourist spots. They asked whether I got training with the Pakistani intelligence services, the Inter-Services Intelligence (ISI). They said everyone they had asked had been able to bring back papers so why had I failed to do my job? No one in the past had got caught. I said I had agreed to do the work out of my patriotism. But I was too scared to carry out the work. It was the simple truth which they refused to believe.

It was a pleasure seeing a nice clean room, a carpet on the floor and furniture. But I was soon taken downstairs. This time when I entered the room I immediately got the rancid smell of the stale air. I felt some vital decision about my future was being taken upstairs. I felt fear in the pit of my stomach and it did not make it any better to hear the cries of pain from the next room.

I had to sit facing the wall. I wondered who these people were who kept asking me the same questions again and again. I wondered what would happen to me. That night Subhash Tandon came and told the other policemen 'Let us take him and finish him off.' I got really scared. At that time I had not heard of false encounters but I felt they were getting ready to finish me off because I had seen their faces and I could identify them.

I was blindfolded and my hands were tied behind me. It was dark, and late at night. I was bundled into a vehicle. I could not hear any other vehicle. I heard one of them ask: 'Have you taken your katta?' I was not sure what a 'katta' meant but it sounded like a weapon. Then they stopped the vehicle and someone ordered the others to take me down. But even after the vehicle had stopped moving they did not take me out.

The officer said this was the last chance I had to tell the truth about the papers. I repeated my story and asked them to take me back to my parents. Then there was silence. I asked them to let me go. They told me to shut up. Finally, I was brought back to the room.

Next day they came with a lot of blank papers and told me to sign them. They warned that my signature should match the signature on my passport. I knew it is wrong and dangerous to sign on blank pieces of paper. I do not know how I found the strength to protest and refused to sign. I asked what they intended to do with the papers. I was wondering what they could do with them. I did not have any land which they could take away through fraud. Nothing else occurred to me.

I stubbornly refused to sign the papers. Now, I wonder how I did that because I actually thought they were going to kill me. They brought some instruments and started pulling out the nail of my toe. Blood came out. I screamed but did not sign. Then they grabbed my left hand after asking which hand I used for writing. My tormentors threatened to pull out the nails one by one till I signed all the papers. I could still hear the screams from the other room. I did not want to think what they were doing to the man.

I signed and signed and signed. There must have been at least 100 to 150 blank pages. Then they brought four or five diaries with dates. I was made to write in Urdu. I was told to write only on certain dates. I did not understand the meaning of what I was writing. For instance, I was told to write something like this: '*Maine Sadar Bazar parties ko maal diya. Imam sahib se mulaqat ki aur do parti ko maal diya.*' There was an Islamic Diary in which they told me to write the names of various chemicals. I had no idea what this was all about.

Then the same men who had tortured me put balm on my wounds and massaged me with oil. I started getting better food. The bread was not stale and the rotis were not burnt. I could eat as many rotis as I liked and once I remember I ate ten in one go.

I could not understand this change in behaviour.

But their talk continued to be as vulgar and communal as before even if it was not as violent.

Then suddenly one day they gave me a bath and a barber was called to give me a shave and cut my hair. On the morning of 28 February they gave me breakfast and gave me another bath. They gave me the clothes that I had worn when I was kidnapped. Pant, shirt and chappals.

I was taken out without blindfold. My eyes hurt because I had not seen the sun for so many days. They took my photos from different angles, my hand- and footprints. I said I was not a criminal so why was I being treated as one. They said 'You won't understand, it is all for your good.'

I was taken to a big white vehicle and found other prisoners already sitting inside it. The policemen were now in uniform. My face was covered with a cloth except for my eyes. The other people also had a cloth on their faces. We were like slaves, not prisoners.

They told me to keep my eyes focused on the floor of the van. Before taking me to the van I was warned to keep quiet, 'Don't say anything about the beating because you will have to come back here. We will pick up your parents.' The thought that these vile people could harm my Ammi and Abbu gave rise to a deep fear in the pit of my stomach.

Just as the vehicle started to move one of the

policemen shouted '*Jai*' and the rest answered in unison— '*Bajrang Bali ki*'. It was as if they were going to war.

NOTES

1. A jallaad is a flayer, executioner, but is also used to mean a person who has no mercy.
2. Aamir found out the names of the officers, including Subhash Tandon only when he saw them in uniform with their name tags at the Inter-State Cell of the Crime branch at Chanakyapuri, New Delhi and at the courts. The court records show that the following officers of the Inter-State Cell Crime Branch were involved in the investigation and interrogation of Aamir—Inspector Subhash Tandon, Inspector Rajinder Bhatia, SI Rakesh Dixit, SI Anil Dureja, ASI Virendra Singh and ASI Ramesh Kumar. They all appeared as prosecution witnesses.

4

HOW I WAS INSIDIOUSLY FRAMED

~

'The police told me that I had to admit to being involved in bomb blasts...that I had to admit to the charges and since the case was false I would come out in a few years. When I resisted I was beaten. I was made to lie on my stomach and my legs and arms were pulled together. It was very painful and my back hurt very badly. Then they put a rod under the knees and sat on my legs. They really broke both my body and my spirit.'

I did not know where we were going. It must have been a fifteen- or twenty-minute ride, after which the vehicle pulled into the compound of a large building. All of us were handcuffed so we had to be helped to climb down; I could see a lot of people and policemen were present. We were taken through the crowd into the building. They made us walk fast. We stopped outside one room where our handcuffs were removed and we entered the room. A person was sitting on a high seat and next to him a man was typing away furiously. Behind the man in the high seat a photo of Gandhiji was hanging on the wall.

I was trying to understand where I was. I had never seen such a scene. One of the policemen started speaking in English, which I could not understand. The police officer put various things in front of the man sitting on a high chair including papers, files, bundles and a revolver. There was a man dressed like a lawyer also speaking in English.

The man on the high seat threw a glance at us. We were all standing at the back of the room. Then he spoke to the lawyer and police officer. All this was in English. Suddenly it occurred to me that I was inside a court. Scenes from a Hindi film I had seen flashed through my mind. In the film the judge asks Amitabh Bachchan to explain how he escaped and Amitabh tells the police and guards to stand aside and make space for him—then he escapes!

We were taken out of the room. The policemen looked pleased and I heard one of them say they had got ten days' 'remand'. I did not understand exactly what the word meant but it sounded ominous enough to send a shiver down my back. Then to my surprise I saw a huge group of people with cameras and mikes. They were men and women from the television channels. They surrounded us. One man tried to elbow himself towards me and asked '*Aise tumne kyu kiya?*' I wondered what I had done. And again I felt a rising fear.

All of us remained silent. We were like robots following orders. We were quickly ushered into the vehicle. The driver kept honking to make space and get away from the media. I could not make out what was happening.

Again we were told to keep our gaze on the floor of the vehicle. I noticed that when we were being brought to the court the policemen looked very tense, but now they were relaxed and almost triumphant.

All of us were taken to the building which I later learnt was the Inter-state Crime Cell at Chanakyapuri. We were fourteen to fifteen persons. Two policemen accompanied each one and led us away to different rooms.

I was put back in the cell where I had been tortured. I thought they would start the torture again. I began to think that I would be here forever and the judge would believe them and not even try to find out my real story. The suspense of not knowing what would happen next was killing me.

For the next ten days I was kept in the same room and the verbal abuse and communal comments continued. One day a soft-spoken officer came and talked to me at length. He told me the story of how Parsis had come to India after they were persecuted in Iran. When they came to Gujarat in a ship and asked permission to settle there, the ruler sent them a full glass of milk to indicate that there was no room for them. The Parsis mixed sugar in the glass and returned it to indicate that they would mix with the local population and live as one. Then the ruler allowed them to enter and ever since they have lived peacefully in India.

I had never heard of the Parsis so I found the story interesting but I could not understand why he told it to me or how it had any bearing on my situation. My ancestors had come from Afghanistan but had chosen to make India their home; my father had never supported the idea of Pakistan and I had been born in the galis of Old Delhi. I knew no other home. So, how was the story of the Parsis relevant to me?

In the night I was taken to the Chanakyapuri Police Station and put in the lock-up for the night. I was put in along with one or two men who had also been produced in the court along with me. Apart from these two there were two others who appeared to be criminals. We were given blankets which were stinking and there was no water in the toilet.

I wanted to speak to the other prisoners but we were ordered to stay apart and not speak to each other. And the criminals were also told not to speak to us.

The next morning they took us back to the rooms in the Inter-state Crime Cell.

It was here that the police told me that I had to admit to being involved in bomb blasts. They told me I had to admit to the charges and since the case was false I would come out in a few years.[1] When I resisted I was beaten. I was made to lie on my stomach and my legs and arms were pulled together and joined in an arch. It was very painful and my back hurt very badly.

Then they put a rod under the knees and sat on my legs. Even now I have pain in my knees. They really broke both my body and my spirit. I knew that from now on I would have to accept whatever they said. I even began to feel I had done wrong by throwing the bag at the Wagah railway station and this was a punishment I was getting for a wrong I had committed. They told me that if I ever wanted to meet my family again I must accept whatever they said.

Almost every day different people came to question me. I do not know who they were because they did not introduce themselves. Before they came, the police would tell me some story about how I had planted a bomb somewhere or the other and I was supposed to repeat it to those people. I could not make very much sense of what was happening.

One day I was allowed to have a bath and given new clothes. I was taken upstairs and there I saw my parents, accompanied by Abbu's friend, Chawla Saheb. I was taken into the room but Chawla Saheb had to remain outside. Abbu was wearing a kurta-pyjama. He just asked: '*Kya hua, beta? Yeh sab kaise hua?*'

Ammi was wearing a burqa and she hugged me and tried to press my arm to find out whether I was okay. She burst into tears and I was terrified that they had arrested my parents as they had threatened to do during the interrogations.

The police had told me to tell them I was involved in the blasts but the meeting was so brief that there was no time; they had to leave. They had got permission from the court to meet me after they read in the papers that I had been arrested in connection with the bomb blasts in Delhi in 1997. I could only tell them not to worry and that I would explain everything later: '*Baad mey bataoonga, abhi sab theek hai. Aap phikr na kare.*' My parents asked permission from the police to give me a copy of the Quran Sharif. The police took it and said they would give it to me but they never did. I did not have the courage to ask them for it.

Chawla Saheb smiled at me as I was led past him. Sultan Ahmed Chawla was educated and a businessman from the Qaum-e-Punjabian community. My parents must have gone to him for advice because he was educated and a businessman so he knew a little about the law. I understood that he must have helped them reach me.

I cannot remember the exact dates of the events that took place during the days I spent in remand. I was remanded to police custody on 28 February 1998 and it was on 26 April 1998 that I was sent to Tihar Jail.

Looking back now, I realize the police were using this time to frame me in various blast cases. When my remand in one case was over they took me to court and got remand for another ten days and I was taken to another police station. I cannot even remember how many times I was produced before a magistrate; none of the magistrates asked me any questions about the circumstances of my arrest.

I was repeatedly produced before the magistrates in the Tis Hazari courts. Every time I was produced in the court for remand my parents were present; but I was not allowed to say even a few words to them or to hug Ammi. It was really distressing to see Ammi cry with tears flowing down her cheeks.

Abbu arranged for a lawyer and paid him Rs 5,000 for each appearance. I knew he could ill-afford to pay such large sums of money. The lawyer did not have much of a role; on one occasion when he did try to raise an objection to some disclosure statements that I was supposed to have signed, the judge did not listen.[2] It seemed the magistrates had all decided I was guilty without giving me an opportunity to say anything in my defence.

It was not only in the courts that I was being pronounced guilty. Every time the police took me for a medical check-up,[3] they would tell the doctors that I was the one responsible for the bomb blasts in Delhi and the doctor would not bother to examine me. On one occasion, a Sikh doctor even told the police accompanying me: '*Isko theek kyoo nahi kiya. Hum hain na.*' Imagine a doctor telling the police to beat a man and say that he was willing to give them a false certificate.

Only once did a doctor do her duty. It was a lady doctor. I do not know her name but it was in the Ram Manohar Lohia Hospital. She made the policemen take off my handcuffs and insisted they leave the room even when the policemen told her I was a dangerous terrorist. After the policemen left she told me to sit on the stool and asked me whether I had been tortured. I did not dare complain. Besides, even though she made me take off my shirt and checked my arms and legs and back to look for any signs of beating, there were none.[4] In any case if she wrote anything against the police I would have to suffer the consequences. I said I was all right.

Slowly I began to realize how serious the cases were against me and how the police were trying to prepare witnesses to testify against me. After the initial ten days' remand, the court gave another remand to the Special Cell at Lodhi Road so I was moved to the Lodhi Road police station; from there I was taken to Roop Nagar police station. One policeman, Heera Malik, was completely drunk and obviously hated Muslims. He hit me because I was a Muslim and said he would make sure that I would be convicted in his case.

Then the Criminal Investigation Department of Haryana got my remand and took me to Sonepat and Rohtak in Haryana. Their language was very harsh and they beat me very badly. In Sonepat I saw torture equipment (stocks) where a number of men could be shackled in one row. Apparently it was used during the Mughal times because the policemen told me: '*Tumhare zamane ka hai. Mughal zamane ka hai.*'

(These are from your time, Mughal times). Obviously, they associated Mughal rule with Muslims and since I was a Muslim, in their eyes I was somehow responsible for the torture carried out by the Mughals.

From Sonepat I was taken back to the Inter-state Crime Cell in Delhi. There I was introduced to a man from Uttar Pradesh called Shakeel who lived in Pilkhuwa village in Ghaziabad and two Bangladeshis, Mousa and Abdullah. In the lock-up I was able to speak to Shakeel and I discovered that he had been arrested before me and kept in detention for much longer. He was a feriwala, a hawker, who sold printed bedsheets and bedcovers. He looked broken and he limped. Shakeel was some ten to twelve years older than me.

The Bangladeshis could not speak Urdu fluently. They were construction labourers working in Ludhiana when they were arrested and since then they had been kept in detention for over a month. They kept close together. The policemen made the Bangladeshis clean the place, wash clothes and utensils. I could see that they too had been tortured.

One evening it was drizzling and I was at the Inter-state Crime Cell. I was told that some people would be coming to see me and I must tell them I was responsible for the blasts in Karol Bagh in an eatery called Roshan Di Kulfi. The police told me to say that I had placed a bomb on a thela (handcart) near that place. They warned that if I failed to do so I would be tortured again.

They took me upstairs to the first floor. I saw three or four people sitting there. I was told to sit on the floor and then ask those people for their forgiveness. I noticed that the people had burn marks on their faces. They were white scars. I realized that they were the victims of the bomb blasts and they had suffered injuries. One of the victims asked me why I had done such a terrible act against innocent people. I wanted to cry out and tell them I had not done it. I would never even think of doing such a heinous crime.

But the memory of the pain and humiliation of the torture was fresh and I told the people sitting before me that I had put the bombs in Karol Bagh and asked them to forgive me.[5] I was made to make similar false confessions to other people as well.

Then the police took me to the bazar and made me point out certain shops and say I had bought chemicals from them to make bombs. The shopkeepers were angry and asked if I had any receipts. The police made the shopkeepers give false receipts. Later, in court the police were exposed because one of the shopkeepers had put the date of that day in 1998—on the same paper where, on the top, the police had put a day in 1997.

At the Lodhi Road police station of the Special Cell there was a one-way glass where the witnesses could see me but I could not see them. They were asked to look at my face carefully and say whether they had seen me on the day of the bomb blast. I was terrified that someone would say they had seen me—after all, so many months had passed. Seeing my anxiety, a Muslim havaldar in the police station told me that the witnesses had already identified me.

Then one day Shakeel and I were taken to Pilkhuwa village of Ghaziabad. Shakeel was from a very poor family with a wife and three children dependent on him. The police said he was a neighbour of Tunda,[6] a militant who was now based in Pakistan. The police called three or four people and told them to say they had sold chemicals to us for making bombs. All those people refused to say they had sold chemicals to either Shakeel or me.

Another man with a beard was the landlord of the room which was rented by Shakeel for printing bedsheets and bedcovers. Shakeel's landlord was told to say that I had stayed with Shakeel and used to come and go. The man refused to make false accusations. He categorically said he did not know me but the police made him sign on blank pieces of paper.

I do not remember the exact day on which Holi was celebrated that year but the policemen were very happy on that day and distributed sweets. They told me they had got promotions and that was their award for arresting me and three others. They would be getting cash awards for their good work.[7]

On 28 April 1998, I found myself in the blue jail vehicle. Inside the vehicle were three long planks which served as benches for the prisoners. I got a seat in a corner from where I watched the other prisoners getting in. The thing I most remember is the foul smell that emanated from their bodies. There were some who seemed to have their seats reserved and if someone sat on their seats, he was roughed up. There were fights and finally many prisoners did not get any seat at all— they stood all the way to Tihar Jail.

It did not seem as if the prisoners were going to jail. They were laughing and joking amongst themselves. I was watching all this with my heart in my mouth. What kind of world would I be entering? The question kept gnawing at my innards.

The only picture of a jail that came to my mind was the one I had seen in the Bollywood movies. Perhaps it was in *Sholay* or was it some other film where Amitabh Bachchan is seen breaking stones in the hot sun. Would I also have to do that?

The vehicle started off. The windows had bars and wire-meshing so I could not see the route the vehicle was taking. Inside the van there was a lot of noise. But

I saw there were others who were also going to jail for the first time and they, like me, sat quietly with frightened expressions on their faces.

When we reached we entered through massive gates and I saw another set of uniformed men who were the jail authorities. The vehicle stopped. The guard called out some names and those people got down. And the vehicle started off again. This time we went on the road inside the jail complex and on both sides were pink walls. I could not see beyond those walls.

Then our vehicle finally stopped at Jail No. 5.[8] They called out my name and I got up and moved to the vehicle door, stepped down and found myself entering through a small door which was a part of the massive gate. Across from where I entered there was another massive gate.

In between these two massive gates, one opened into the outside world and the other into the jail. In the middle there was a large space where we were all told to squat on the floor. Later I learnt this space is called 'deodhi' by the inmates. I noticed that the keys in the hands of the policeman were huge. He used one massive key to bolt the door from which we had entered.

We were asked whether we had any knives, money or any other belongings; no one got up. The guards were all dark complexioned and we discovered they were from Tamil Nadu Special Police (TSP). The Delhi Armed Police and Delhi Jail police were also there.

We, the new entrants, were told to go up the stairs on the left. It was a strange silence. The only sound was the man calling out names. Sometimes I heard the sound of the bolt opening and closing. Otherwise there was absolute silence. We prisoners were absolutely silent. I think it was the silence of fear.

We sat till the evening. Little by little our curiosity got the better of us and there were some whispered conversations. A man in front of me asked me my name and what my case was. When I said I had been booked in a bomb blast case he whispered, 'Which bomb blast?' I replied I had no idea because I had not been involved in any bomb blasts. He informed me that I would be put into the high-risk ward. He told me he had been caught for theft and this was not his first time.

I asked him what kind of food we would get and he said it was okay although it was not quite like home food. I asked him whether they beat the prisoners. He said they do but not as much as at the police station. He said they beat the convicts more than the undertrial prisoners.

Finally the doctor came. We had been waiting for our medical examination. Along with him came two men dressed in white khadi kurta-pyjamas and white topis. My informant told me they were convicts who assisted the jail authorities. He also told me they would call out my name and ask questions. If I did not answer promptly I would be slapped.

I managed to answer the questions without inviting any slaps. They took my height and weight. The doctor asked me what I was in for and when I said it was for a bomb blast he was a bit taken aback. I assured him I had not done it.

After the medical examination I was told to climb down the stairs and go to the other side. It was next to the meeting room where prisoners met their relatives. Next to that was a room full of files. These files were called warrants. There I discovered that I had been called Aamir alias Kamran alias Guddu alias Imran. I protested that I did not have any other names but the man in charge said these names had been put by the police. He read out the cases against me and the jail officer commented that my warrant was really big. It was then I began to realize that they had put many cases against me. I still did not know how many.

I went downstairs. The TSP told us to sit down. I noticed they were much politer than other forces. They did not hit for small things. They did a thorough body search but I was not subjected to a cavity search. If they suspected anyone of smuggling something then they would put on gloves and even search the prisoner's rectum.

The security guard had the keys of the other side gate. He opened the massive lock and bolt and told me to step inside. He pointed to a tower in the middle and ordered: 'Go to the chakkar.'

The jail building was a new one in a semi-circular shape and I could see that the wards had numbers. It was quite different from what I expected. There was a garden full of flowers. The chakkar was the control room from where the jail authorities kept a watch on all the wards. I saw a young man was being beaten up at the chakkar and I felt a sudden fear. He was screaming but I did not understand why he was being beaten. Again we were called one by one and asked our particulars, which were written down in a huge register.

When my turn came, the officer looked at me and asked how I could be involved in such a big case. I again repeated that I was innocent. I told them my whole story. My warrant was lying on the table. One officer said I should be sent to the high-risk ward or high-security ward.[9]

There was a doctor there who said I was too young to be kept by myself in a cell. The jail officer argued that I was accused in very serious cases and I was a terrorist. However, the doctor said he would not take the responsibility for sending me to that ward. While they argued they told me to sit at a distance. Finally, a convict came and took me took to Ward No. 5 just behind the chakkar. I learnt that it was the Mulahiza Ward for young prisoners and first-timers.[10]

Again my particulars were taken. I looked around at the barrack. There were no beds. In one corner there was a toilet and bathroom. There was only half a door so you could be seen at all times. There was a light bulb which was on and a fan. The convict who had brought me asked whether I had eaten. When I said I had not, he pointed to the food.

I took a thali and helped myself to the dal from a bucket and took some rotis. The dal had a peculiar smell and I could not swallow the food. But I forced myself to drink water. I poured out water from an earthenware pot into a dirty plastic glass and drank it.

For a long time I sat staring out of the bars and finally I fell asleep on the smelly blanket. It was my first night in jail.

NOTES

1. The police knew that Aamir was being framed and thought that the cases would be proved false in the courts.
2. Confessions or disclosure to the policemen are inadmissible evidence under the Indian criminal law. And the police is not allowed to make the accused sign any statement. The reason for this is to protect the

accused from being convicted on the basis of false confessions extracted from the accused by torture.

3. Under the Criminal Procedure Code, the police must take the accused for a medical check-up every forty-eight hours during the time he is under their custody. This is another procedural safeguard against torture.
4. The torture is conducted in a way that there are no obvious marks left but often there are long-term health consequences. For instance, the roller treatment can lead to kidney damage; the voltage and current can be controlled with precision while giving electric shocks used to cause pain and fear without physically harming the victim's body.
5. At the time an organization calling itself the Shaheed Khalsa claimed responsibility for the blasts but the police claimed Pakistan's Inter-Services Intelligence agency masterminded the explosions. Immediately after the blast, three Kashmiri men were arrested in connection with these blasts. The question is, what happened to those men? See: http://m.rediff.com/news/oct/27blast1.htm.
6. Syed Abdul Karim Tunda is alleged to be an operative of the Lashkar-e-Toiba; called Tunda after he lost his left hand in a bomb-making accident.
7. It is still unclear how they got the cash award when they had already arrested three Kashmiri men on the same charges a year ago. The names of the three arrested men were: Mohammed Shafi Dhobi alias Yusuf Khan, Abdul Ahad Bhatt alias Mohammed

Yunuf Bhatt and Abdul Rashid Najjar alias Maqbool. See: http://m.rediff.com/news/oct/27blast1.htm.

8. Tihar is South Asia's largest prison complex with nine prisons within the complex; Jail No. 5 is for young prisoners between the age of eighteen and twenty-one.
9. The ward meant for prisoners accused of crimes relating to terrorism where the men are often kept in isolation. It is also called Highlight in jail parlance.
10. The Mulahiza Ward had ten barracks of which Barracks 2 and 3 were for new entrants; all of them were full beyond their capacity.

5

PROVING MY INNOCENCE

~

'I could not sleep that night. The faces of the victims of the blasts kept floating by and I decided that when I was released I would seek them out and tell them the truth about how the police had kidnapped me and tortured me.'

The next morning I tried eating the jail meals but I could not make myself swallow the food. But by dinner time I was so hungry I ate the vegetables even though I saw worms in the dish. I found out that there was a canteen within the jail where we could buy basic necessities such as soap, toothpaste and hair oil. There was also another canteen which sold tea and snacks such as samosas and jalebis. But I did not have money. I desperately needed a new set of clothes. The only clothes I had were the ones I was wearing on the day the police kidnapped me when I was on my way to buy medicine.

I knew Abbu and Ammi would eventually find their way to the jail so I waited anxiously when the nambardars came to call out the names for the mulaqaats, or meetings. A nambardar was a convict who had the privilege of assisting the jail authorities. He would come to each ward and call out: '*Han bhai mulaqaat sun lo.*' We would all gather around him and wait for the lucky ones who had visitors. It was one of the two ways we got news of the outside world; the second was when we were taken to the court.

It was in the first week of May that I heard my name called out. I could not believe it so I asked whether he had really called out my name. I was so happy. I had not met Abbu or Ammi since my arrest, except for the brief encounter during the time I was in remand; at the court I had got just a glimpse of them. We had hardly spoken to each other.

It took almost an hour to finish the formalities before I could reach the mulaqaat room. I had to register my name at the chakkar and then at the deodhi. The mulaqaat room was very noisy. There were so many prisoners crushed together in the hall and we could not see clearly through the wire mesh and grilles. I went close to the grilles and spotted Ammi and Abbu through the wire mesh. On seeing them I burst into tears. My mother saw me and she too could not stop her tears. Abbu stood stoically looking at me. Ammi wanted to know how I was, whether I had good food.

Abbu told me to control myself and then asked in a voice full of pain—pain born of shame: '*Kya hua, kaise hua?*' This was the first time I could actually speak to them. There was a huge crowd so we had to talk very loudly. People were listening to us, both visitors and the prisoners. But I told them what had happened.

Abbu looked so frail; he had aged and his shoulders were drooping. But he assured me that he believed in my innocence and he would make sure that I was defended by a lawyer who would get me acquitted. He said he would pray for me and fight for me.

Abbu informed me that he was finding it difficult to get a good lawyer, especially one whose fees he could afford. But he said Chawla Saheb had suggested an advocate named Feroze Khan Ghazi. The advocate was from our community, a Pathan, and he was involved in helping the community through social work.

Then Ammi informed me that she had given my passport and all my certificates and identity cards to the person with whom I had sent a letter. She said a man called Mohammad Ali had come with my letter. I realized that the police had tricked her into handing over all my documents. Ammi had kept the letter but it was never used as evidence to prove that the police version of my arrest was a blatant lie.

There was so much more to discuss but the bell began ringing and our meeting was over. Abbu gave me Rs 200, some clothes and fruits. In the jail we were not given cash but the cash deposited was converted into coupons which we could spend for buying things from the two canteens.

I still did not know what I was being accused of; how the police had framed me. I did not have to wait too long. In May the police filed the charge sheet against me. I read the charge sheet and was shocked by the lies it contained. The First Information Report (FIR) was filed on 27 February 1998. Obviously, there was no record of the way I had been kidnapped by the police and tortured for eight days.

According to the charge sheet the Inter-state Cell of the Crime Branch was carrying out an investigation in connection with the bomb blasts which took place in Delhi in 1997 when they got intelligence reports that the contacts of Pakistan-based terrorist Abdul Karim alias Tunda used to hide in House No. 1001 Anarwali Gali Teliwala Dilli. So a strict watch was kept on the house.

That was Abbu's address. I noticed there were no details from when such a watch had been kept, who kept the watch and how 'the activities' in our home had aroused suspicion.

The charge sheet continued the police story:

> While watching the house the police found two men emerging from the house. The men walked towards the Sadar Bazar railway station via Azad market. They reached near Signal no. 10 when one man stopped to urinate and he saw the police party and the two started going faster when they were nabbed. The two men were from Bangladesh. They took out their pocket diaries and tore some sheets and put it in their mouths.
>
> Both had bags hanging from their shoulders in which hand grenades (one in each bag) were found. There and then on arrest the two told the police that they had come to India on the 'ishara' of Abdul Karim alias Tunda alias Abdul Qadoos whose left hand is amputated. They also told the police that

they were in touch with Tunda who told them to carry out a jihad in Delhi, Haryana, Punjab and UP. They said they would be meeting a young man in front of the Hanifi masjid near the Sadar Bazar railway station at six-thirty in the evening.

Acting on this information the police waited at the appointed time and saw a man by the name of Mohammad Aamir Khan alias Qamran alias Imran alias Abbu Akasa alias Umar come out of a mosque. He was accompanied by Mohammad Shakeel alias Hamza, son of Sulieman, resident of 235 Sherwali Gali, Ashok Nagar, Pilkhua, Ghaziabad.

Aamir was searched and a revolver and live cartridges were found on him. He was carrying a briefcase in which there were various certificates, passports and five diaries. On interrogating Mohammad Aamir Khan they discovered that: '...because Mohammad Aamir Khan's sister Chaman is married to someone in Pakistan he went to visit her and while he was there he went to a masjid where he was influenced by the sermons which were against India and about the atrocities done on Muslims and inspired the men to join the jihad against India. That is how Mohammad Aamir joined the jihad against India. He got 'daur-e-aam' and 'daur-e-khas' training and then he came in contact with Abdul Karim alias Tunda who gave him training in bomb making. He was fully trained, that is why Abdul Karim included him in the jihad against India. In Delhi he was given

> a contact, Amaar of Cheechawatni, a Pakistani who told Aamir to meet him and start and continue the jihad. Before going to Delhi he was given contacts of existing organizations' names and addresses and also contacts for Pakistan and also various formula for making bombs and codenames for cities and codenames for various chemicals. Imam Sahib code for potassium chloride, badam rogan for nitro benzene.'[1]

According to the police I got radicalized while I was in Karachi on my visit to my sister and thereafter got training so how come I had planted all those bombs without training and without contact with the radical elements before going to Pakistan? It was obviously a blatantly untrue story. But would the police accept that?

I wondered how my lawyer was going to prove that the police had just made up all these lies.

The argument on charges came up for hearing one whole year later in the Tis Hazari.[2] On that day there were twenty men who stood accused in this case. Of these twenty, which included me, two men were from well-off families, educated families. One was Abdul Baqi. He too had been kidnapped but since his parents were educated they had immediately sent off telegrams to various authorities that their son was missing. These telegrams were proof that their son had been picked up long before the date shown of his official arrest. He had a good lawyer who argued that there was no evidence of any recovery from him and the man was discharged.

The other man who also came from a well-off family owned a garage. His name was Shamim Akhtar and he came from some place in West Bengal. When we saw his lawyer we were amazed. His family knew a judge in Kolkata who got him a lawyer from the Supreme Court. When the lawyer started arguing, there was silence. Everyone was listening to him with rapt attention and the other lawyers noted the precedents he quoted; even the judge sat up and the public prosecutor showed deference to him. The lawyer, whose name I have forgotten, had very good assistants. Shamim Akhtar was discharged at this time of all charges. Because of his lawyer three others were also discharged.

I saw that there was a possibility of justice. But I also realized that it depended so much on the quality of arguments of the advocate. Abbu went to the lawyer to ask whether he would do my case but when he named his fees Abbu felt really upset because he knew he could not afford to pay that kind of money. Besides, even if he managed to raise the money for the fee for one case, the problem was that there were altogether nineteen cases against me.

The police claimed that I had disclosed to them that I was involved in the bomb blasts of 1997 during the period I was in remand. It was on the basis of my disclosure statements that I had been charged with bombing various places in Delhi, Sonepat, Rohtak and Ghaziabad. All the bomb blasts took place before I had been to Pakistan. No one noticed the holes in the police story. But my lawyers told me that disclosure statements were not admissible evidence. I did not understand the finer points of criminal law. I just knew I was innocent and if there was any justice then I should have been discharged.

Feroze Khan Ghazi assured Abbu that the evidence against me was weak and I would ultimately be acquitted; it was a question of time.

Abbu dedicated his life to getting me justice. After coming out of jail, when I was looking through his papers preserved by Ammi, I found dozens of small slips of paper on which he would write the court dates on which the various cases were to come up. Some of these slips are actually the reverse side of the bus tickets. Reading the slips, I realized that in the first few years I was brought to court three to four times a week in connection with some proceeding or the other in the nineteen cases. Abbu was always there.

Abbu arrived before the courts opened. He went straight to the typists who sit in rows outside the lawyers' chambers. They make money typing simple applications. He came early so he could get his applications typed. The application was to the concerned judge, usually for permission to meet me in the lock-up; many a time it was an application to get the court's permission to give me home-made food or some other miscellaneous application. Ghazi Saheb did not have time to attend to such details. Abbu had to pay several hundred rupees to the typists for each application.

Armed with his application, Abbu made his way through the crowds to the court where my case would come up. He waited for the case to come up, he waited for the lawyer to appear and he waited to catch a glimpse of me.

Then after the court proceedings, Abbu would try and meet me in the court lock-up and carry messages back and forth from me to my lawyer who had little time to talk to me. Many times Ammi would accompany him. While it was reassuring to see my parents there, it was also very painful because I could see the tension and strain was telling on them.

At the time I did not know the extent of the tensions Abbu and Ammi were facing. The police constantly harassed them and frequently visited them in their home. As a result our neighbours got scared and no one dared to visit my parents. When I came out of jail, my advocate Feroze Khan Ghazi told me he had once gone with Abbu to offer namaaz at the local mosque. He noticed that no one returned his greetings and slunk away after the prayers so they did not have to face him.

It really makes me so angry and also so dejected when I think of how alone my parents were during the whole time I was in jail. I blame the leaders of our community, the Muslim leaders most of all, because they should have understood my parents' anguish; especially my mother's agony when she was left alone after my father's death. She must have been so alone, terrified and vulnerable.

No one came forward to offer any financial help or even to accompany her as she went on her rounds from court to jail and from jail to the lawyers.

In July 2000, Abbu wrote a formal complaint to the District Commissioner of Police (DCP) North about the harassment by the police. I saw a copy of the complaint after I was released. Abbu wrote that the police had been regularly coming to our house, both in uniform and in civil dress; they also called him to the police station. Abbu complained that the police 'used to abuse me in unprintable language'.

The immediate provocation for writing the complaint was that Abbu was called to the Bara Hindu Rao police station at 9.30 in the morning on 4 July

2000 and threatened. He wrote: 'I was threatened by the police of being implicated in false cases if I continue to meet my son in the jail or in the court.'

Apparently, the harassment did lessen but my parents found themselves totally isolated and alone at a time they needed the help of neighbours, relatives and friends the most.

In November 2000 while I was in Jail No. 3 an incident happened that had far-reaching effects on my mental and physical health. I was going to the toilets one morning when suddenly I was attacked by a convict, Vijay Kumar, a dismissed constable of the Delhi police. He attacked me for no reason. He bashed me up using his fists and elbows. I screamed for help and I could see that the warden was standing by watching. The warden whose name was Sanjeev, did not intervene. Instead he shouted: '*Maro saale is deshdrohi ko*' (Beat the bastard—traitor to his country).

I fell unconscious and when I recovered I found myself in the jail hospital. By this time I had become aware of my rights and insisted on being taken to DDU (Deen Dayal Upadhyaya) hospital outside the jail and registering a MLC (medical legal case). I was in the DDU hospital for the entire day.

When I returned to the jail in the evening, I was shocked to learn that the jail authorities had decided to take action against me on the basis of a complaint filed against me by Vijay Kumar, the man who had assaulted me in front of the warden.[3] I was locked up inside a small cell, called the Kasoori cell.[4]

I was confined inside a small cell in Ward No. 2 twenty-four hours a day for several months. A thick blanket was tied around the bars to block out light and I was deprived of sunshine in the cold winter months. This was also during the holy month of Ramazan so I was keeping fasts.

I developed high blood pressure and it was from that time my eyesight was affected; I also started suffering from memory loss. It was the worst experience of my entire time in the jail.

It was during the time I was inside the dark cell, deprived of human contact and in complete isolation, that the alarm went off. It sounded like a horn. We had been told that if we heard the horn we must immediately go inside any cell nearest to us, even if it is not ours. Anyone found outside was severely beaten. Being locked inside the dark cell I was terrified, wondering what had provoked this alarm.

Later some prisoners whispered to me that a Muslim prisoner had been killed by the jail authorities in Jail No. 5. It was just a few days after Eid.

Throughout Ramazan I was inside the Kasoori cell. I kept my fasts. A Hindu Gujjar prisoner whose name was Devinder used to secretly throw dates and packets of milk into my cell. It was such acts of solidarity that made our lives in the jail bearable and helped me preserve my humanity.

While I was still inside the Kasoori cell I heard of the terrible earthquake in Gujarat. It was on Republic Day. The jail authorities asked for donations for the quake victims and I contributed Rs 250.[5]

I was in the Kasoori cell for five long, cold winter months. During those months the proceedings in my trials were transferred to the court complex inside Tihar Jail. Now my parents had to come all the way to Tihar Jail instead of going to the courts in Tis Hazari which were nearer to home.

In the midst of this bleak scenario we had some good news. On 30 November 2000 Judge M.S. Sabherwal acquitted me in a bomb blast case. According to the police I had put a bomb in a shop selling lottery tickets in Ballimaran in June 1997. None of the twenty-three witnesses produced by the prosecution, including the public witnesses, said anything that could incriminate me in the case.

The judge said: 'There is absolutely no evidence on the record to show that the accused Amir [sic] Khan had placed any explosive substance in the show case of Mohd Abid Hussain.'

I remember the day I was acquitted; it was the first

time since my arrest that my mother smiled. I thanked the judge by putting my hand on my heart.

Again, on 15 December 2000, I was acquitted by the same judge in a bomb blast case of February 1997 in which a bomb had been placed in Murliwala Kuan in the Sabzi Mandi area. My co-accused had already been discharged in April 1999. In this case the prosecution produced thirty-eight witnesses and after hearing their testimonies the judge concluded: 'A perusal of the testimonies of these witnesses reveals that none of them have supported the prosecution version and they have even not identified the accused and there is absolutely no evidence which could prove the involvement of the accused Amir Khan [sic] in the commission of the offences alleged against him.'

On 18 January 2001, the same judge acquitted both Shakeel and me in another bomb case. In this case Shakeel and I were accused of planting a bomb on 20 June 1997 at around two-thirty in the afternoon on the pavement near the shop of Sunil Sharma who sold chhole bhature in Shop No. 5648 Nai Sarak, Chandni Chowk. In that bomb blast no one was hurt. The fire caused by the explosion was put out by Sunil Sharma and his employees.

The prosecution produced 24 witnesses. The judge observed that: 'A perusal of the statements of the witnesses examined by the prosecution shows that they have not stated anything against the accused persons, which could connect them with the commission of the offences alleged against them. All the public witnesses have not supported the version of the prosecution and none of them had identified any of the accused persons.'

Some of the prosecution witnesses refused to give false testimony against Shakeel or me even though they had been tutored by the police. These witnesses were declared hostile and cross-examined. Even in the cross-examination, the shop owner Sunil Sharma categorically denied seeing either me or Shakeel pretending to eat chhole bhature at his shop.

The fourth acquittal came on 15 February 1997 in which I was supposed to have put a bomb in Gali Matkewali in Chawri Bazar. Shakeel, my co-accused, had been discharged in February 1999. The prosecution produced 40 witnesses but could not prove their false case against me.

The next acquittal came on 23 March 2001. In this case too Shakeel, my co-accused had been discharged. The prosecution produced 37 witnesses. The first prosecution witness was Tilak Ram Singh, a man who was injured in the blast. The court order acquitting me recorded that Ram Singh 'denied the suggestion that on 10/10/97 he had disclosed the description of a boy who had planted the bomb near the water radii[6]

[sic]. He also denied that he was called to the P S Bara Hindu Rao and had identified the accused person who was standing near the radii, at about 8 p.m. and was having a bomb [sic] containing a bomb.'

This was the case in which the judge decided to record my statement under Section 313[7] before acquitting me on 23 March 2001. This was the first opportunity I got to tell my story to the court.

Ever since the trials began, I had wanted to tell the judge my story but my lawyer told me I would get an opportunity only at the end of the trial. But the trials had finished and I had not been given an opportunity. My lawyer did not have time to visit me in the jail to explain what was happening and I used to feel very despondent.

I would lie awake at night and often cry myself to sleep. I just saw the lights of the tower and heard the sound of the boots of the guards and I thought my entire life would pass within these walls.

Someone even told me that I would die in jail. There was a man who had become a bit mad. He would bathe and soap himself with his clothes on. He would eat his food sitting next to a drain. They told me I would become mad like him.

But then I told myself I had my parents working hard to get me acquitted and my lawyer who assured me that there was no evidence against me and the cases were weak. Anyway, I was glad to have the opportunity to tell my side of the story to the judge.

I told the judge about Guptaji and how he had framed me because I could not do the task he had assigned to me. The court order recorded that I stated that I have been 'falsely implicated at the instance of one Guptaji of Intelligence Bureau'.

On 30 March 2001 I was acquitted in a bomb blast which took place on 25 February 1997. In this case a prosecution witness stated that he had seen me placing a 'thaila' (bag) in the bus but when he was cross-examined he admitted that the first time he saw me was at the police station and the fact that the statement of that witness was recorded much after the event led the court to observe that no reliance could be placed on his testimony.

In April 2001, I was transferred to Jail No. 1. It was there that for no reason I was beaten very badly; they tied me to a pole and beat me on the soles of the feet. This kind of beating leaves no marks but it is very painful. In jail parlance it is called 'Lakshman jhoola'. This kind of violence is common in the jail. There is also the ever-present threat of the blade-baaz who cuts a man's throat. Once many of us went on a hunger strike against the practice of putting offenders like these (blade-baaz) in the same cell with political prisoners.[8]

I was acquitted in five more cases between April and July 2001. The acquittals gave me hope that I would be released soon and could look after Abbu and Ammi who seemed to be ageing very fast because of the trauma of seeing their son in jail. Abbu said to get justice one had to have hands made of gold (because it was so expensive) and feet made of iron (because there was so much running around to do.)

The judge was also sympathetic and the atmosphere in the court was beginning to feel less harrowing. But the trial took a toll on me, especially if the witnesses looked at me with questions in their eyes as if asking: 'Did you plant the bomb?'

I still remember a young woman, Veena, who came into the court limping. She had got injured in the bomb blasts in the Rani Bagh market on 18 October 1997. In that case the prosecution produced 58 witnesses. Kumari Veena was Prosecution Witness No. 4. When she was asked to identify me, she slowly turned to look towards me and our eyes met. Mine were full of fear and hers held a question in them. Her eyes seemed to be asking me whether I had done the act. And I wanted to shout out loud and clear that I was innocent and that I had been framed. She looked at me and then turned to the judge and said no, she had never seen me before.

I could not sleep that night. The faces of the victims

of the blasts kept floating by and I decided that when I was released I would seek them out and tell them the truth about how the police had kidnapped me and tortured me.

On 17 August 2001, I was acquitted in the Rani Bagh blast case. The judge held: 'Perusal of the entire records thus reveals that there is absolutely no evidence against the accused Amir Khan [sic] which could prove his involvement in the commission of the offences against him.'

That day the judge noticed that Abbu was absent. The judge asked where he was and my advocate, Feroze Khan Saheb told him Abbu had been admitted to hospital. The judge gave me permission to visit him in hospital for an hour.

Escorted by the police I arrived at the Bara Hindu Rao hospital and was taken to where Abbu lay. The doctors said that he needed a surgery and I persuaded him to undergo it even though he was very reluctant.

I still remember his words to me: '*Beta, mai tumhari tarikh pay aa nahi sakaa*.' (Son, I could not be present for your court case.)

Lying in the hospital bed he was worried about me. I looked deep into his eyes but could not say much with the police surrounding me. Our words were unspoken. My mother kissed me on the forehead and her tears never stopped flowing. The one hour was over and the police took me back to the jail.

I remember I was in the court but I do not know which case it was. After the proceedings were over, Feroze Khan Ghazi whispered to me that my father had passed away. Life ebbed out of my body and I felt absolutely numb.

The judge noticed that something was amiss and asked what had happened. When he was told the news he said, 'Don't worry, God will take care of everything.' I do not know how I managed to reach my cell and then I collapsed. I sat surrounded by silence. In the evening when I did not come out as usual, my fellow prisoners came to my cell to find out what had happened. The first to arrive was Sushil Sharma, the man involved in the tandoor case. He sat with me for some time. Next came another fellow prisoner. He was in the cell next to mine. Once I saw him crying out to his gods and cursing them for abandoning him. He had a picture of Hanumanji and he was crying and cursing because the court had rejected his application for bail. He sat with me quietly.

I did not eat that evening and I lay awake. Finally, as night fell and all was silent I broke down. I kept thinking of Abbu. His face, his gestures of love, his concern and his last words to me in hospital.

Who would come to court and follow up with the lawyers? Ammi had come with Abbu but did not understand the court proceedings. In any case she would be in mourning for three months so I would have no mulaqaats. I had never felt so desolate in my life. I felt abandoned and in despair. Even though I had been acquitted in twelve cases, there were seven more cases; and the money had already run out.

NOTES

1. Translated from the original Hindi.
2. Under the Criminal Procedure Code, the charge sheet is supposed to be filed within 90 days of the FIR; and then the court fixes a date to hear arguments on charges. It is at that time the accused pleads guilty or not guilty and the court decides whether there is enough material on record to proceed with the trial. Under the law there is no time limit fixed for arguments on charges but the accused have a right to a fair and speedy trial. By delaying the arguments on charges, Aamir's right to a speedy trial had been violated.
3. Ultimately Aamir was acquitted in the case filed by the jail authorities against him; however, the decision on his complaint case against Vijay Kumar and the jail authorities is still to come. But then he could not pursue the case because he could not afford to pay the lawyer's fees.
4. Kasoori roughly translates as a wrong-doer. The so-called Kasoori cells in Tihar jail are in Ward No. 2 of Tihar Jail No. 3. There are twenty cells in the jail hospital which are also used for those accused of

breaking the jail discipline. The mentally ill are also kept in these cells.

5. In the Gujarat earthquake of January 2001, 20,000 people were killed and 400,000 homes were destroyed. The official website of the Press Information Bureau of the Government of India records that the Union Home Minister, L.K. Advani, was presented a cheque of Rs 5,11,000 by the Director General of Tihar to the Prime Minister's Relief Fund on 8 March 2001 a contribution made by prisoners and jail staff.
6. Perhaps it refers to a hand cart carrying water.
7. After the prosecution has produced its witnesses the accused is allowed to make a statement in which he is asked to reply to each accusation made and give his explanation.
8. The blade-baaz is usually a convict who is skilled in slitting people's throats with an open blade, the kind used by traditional barbers.

6

THE POLITICS OF HATRED

~

'I was really shocked by the attack on our Parliament, but I was also shocked by the way all of us Muslims had come under attack. I had never taken interest in politics but now questions came to my mind about the future of Muslims living in India. Would we always be looked upon with suspicion?'

With the passing away of Abbu, I desperately wanted to come out of jail so I could be with Ammi. I thought I would soon be acquitted in the other cases but two events which occurred at the end of 2001 affected my chances of being free any time soon. I did not immediately realize the impact of the two events would have on my life.

The attacks on the Twin Towers in New York on 11 September and the attack on the Indian Parliament on 13 December changed the attitude of the jail authorities towards Muslim prisoners, especially those accused in cases of terrorism. Those two events even changed the attitude of other prisoners towards Muslims.

Even before those attacks I had encountered communal prejudice, mostly from the jail authorities rather than among the prisoners. In the barrack, the prisoners showed great respect for each other's religions. During the first days in jail when I was in the Mundakhana[1] I came in touch with Hindus, Sikhs and Christians.

In the first days in jail there were three prisoners with whom I shared food and had discussions. One was James who was an accused in a dacoity case in south Delhi; Surendra who was from Agra, I don't remember in what case, but I remember that he could speak Japanese. Surendra was about nineteen years old and even the jail officers talked to him. It was supposed to be a great honour if a jail official talked to a prisoner.

Surendra said he had lived in Japan; I do not know how far that was true but Japanese girls used to come and visit him in jail. Surendra generously offered to introduce me to the Japanese girls. I refused his offer. At that time even talk about girls made me feel embarrassed. One of the jail officers also wanted to be introduced to the Japanese girls

And then there was Manoj who helped the nambardars. Later I found James and Manoj had been told to keep an eye on me. But that did not affect our relationship. After all, I had not done anything illegal and I had nothing to hide. Surendra and Manoj were the first Hindus of my age group I got to know closely; while living in Sadar Bazar I had never had any occasion to make Hindu friends of my age.

Then there a Muslim prisoner called Aarif. We, Muslim undertrial prisoners, offered namaaz together in one corner which we had reserved for ourselves. I noticed that whenever it was namaaz time the Hindu prisoners would lower their voices and switch off the television. The Muslim and Christian prisoners would remain silent if the Hindus were praying or when the Sikhs did their ardas early in the morning.

On certain occasions such as Diwali, Raksha Bandhan and Independence Day, we got better meals with a little more spice and chillies. The dal was less watery and the vegetables were cooked better and we were given one laddu each.

Non-vegetarian food was not allowed in the jail.[2]

We were told that Tihar was an ashram. However, we could buy boiled eggs and omelettes from the canteen. The canteen also had items such as: bread pakora for Rs 5; two cups of tea for Rs 2; chhole bhature for Rs 20; and samosas and jalebis in the evening. There was also a dry canteen from where we could buy toiletries, underwear, postcards, butter, buns, salty biscuits and pickles.

Surendra, James, Suraj, Manoj and I would pool in our money to buy a bottle of pickles or in the summer we would buy lassi or buttermilk from the canteen. In the Mundakhana we were allowed to take our food into the barracks so I asked Ammi to bring food for three or four extra people. The others also shared their food with me. I was really surprised that the parathas that Surendra brought were in the shape of a triangle instead of being round like ours.

Three or four of us would also pool our money and buy cinema tickets for those prisoners who could not afford to do so. At that time they showed films every week. In the beginning I used to buy things from the canteen but after Abbu died I did not waste money on such luxuries.

Later, the jail authorities stopped me from going to the movies and even from participating in the outdoor games saying I was a dangerous criminal. I did not know the rules so I just accepted the punishment without challenging them.

Surendra became close to me after I rescued him from being sexually abused by the convicts. There were many cases of young men being raped by the convicts—I rescued several young men from the clutches of those convicts. The convicts who were working with the administration and the guards would take any young man they fancied and rape him. Sometimes even the constables would take part in these sexual orgies.

I remember Tariq, a young man from Jamshedpur. He was effeminate and vulnerable to sexual exploitation by these convicts. On one occasion I saved him. After that he started sleeping next to me. At first I did not mind but then I found he had started moving closer and closer to me. I told him to keep a distance. The other prisoners teased me saying that here was a man who was much sought after and I was rejecting his advances.

The reason I could rescue these young men was because the convicts were scared of me and so they respected me. I was considered a dangerous terrorist. They saw that I was handcuffed and taken to the court along with the prisoners from the high-security ward in what was called the TADA vehicle.[3]

During my first few years in Tihar Jail, I noticed the Muslim prisoners were allowed to collect together to offer namaaz at the chakkar. Mukhtar Ansari, a politician from east Uttar Pradesh, who was in jail at the time, would have a huge dastarkhan spread and invited all the prisoners, both Hindu and Muslim to join in the Eid party he financed. Subhash Thakur, another prisoner, said to be of the Dawood gang contributed money for iftar.

After the Parliament attack on 13 December 2001, this practice was stopped. We were not allowed to offer namaaz together and the raised platform used for offering namaaz in Jail No. 3 was broken on some pretext but the Hindus were allowed to construct temples inside the wards.

The most difficult thing about being in prison is to keep oneself occupied because the days seem so long and there is nothing to fill them. In those days there were cultural programmes every ten to fifteen days. I was told this was a part of the reforms that were introduced by Kiran Bedi.[4]

Apart from seeing the Ram Lila sometimes I had never seen live performances. So, for me, it was an eye-opener to see plays being staged. Sometimes a play would be put up by the prisoners and sometimes outside actors came. There were orchestras which performed musical events and I really felt much better after attending these functions; it helped to fight the depression which inevitably sets in when a person is cut off from his family and friends.

The most memorable cultural event during my stay in Tihar took place in February of 1999. We were told that Jaspal Bhatti[5] had decided to release his new Punjabi comedy in Tihar Jail. Perhaps he was the first director to do so. Most of us had seen him on television and were excited to learn that we would get an opportunity to see him in person. Even more than the prospect of seeing Jaspal Bhatti Saheb and his film we were excited to learn we would be seeing the hero and heroine of the film.

I was very moved by Jaspal Bhatti's gesture of having a premiere in the jail. I knew that premieres were special days for film-makers although I had never been for any. The fact that he was going to have the first show in the jail meant that he thought of us, prisoners, as human beings and not as some kind of scum to be locked up and forgotten.

The whole atmosphere in the jail was charged with expectation. Finally the day arrived; we waited till the evening with rising excitement. When the time came, we came out of our cells and rushed towards the screen.

I had not been out in the night since my arrest; I had almost forgotten what the open sky looked like at night with stars and the moon shining from high above.

We prisoners sat on the ground. On the chairs sat the guests, the jail officers and their families. There was a massive curtain. The film was called *Mahaul Theek Hai*. Before the film started we were introduced to the hero and heroine. It was a pleasure to see their fresh faces and beautiful clothes. Also I felt a little more human because we were all watching the film together, the jail officials, their families and us. I felt included, a part of a large family.

At least for some time I felt I was free. But I was scared that some criminals might create problems. The thought made me tense. Some of these criminals carried on their criminal activities inside the jail and we all suffered. For instance, they used to inject papayas and bananas with drugs and smuggle them inside; when they were caught the jail authorities stopped all of us from having the fruit. It was just 10 per cent of the inmates who spoiled the atmosphere. Why were we all punished for the acts of a few?

Once the film started I became absorbed in the story. It was a satire on the Punjab police who chase terrorists and criminals. Luckily, there was no disturbance. And after the film I was able to enjoy a few moments of freedom sitting under an open sky and looking up at the stars. Then I rushed back to my cell.

I was no longer in Jail No. 5—I had been transferred to Jail No. 3. I had been transferred in the night and put into a cell by myself. There was a red bulb. I could take four strides lengthwise and three across the width. That is how small the cell was. There was a ventilator right on top. The toilet was behind a brick wall. Through the bars I could see another gate and beyond that the ground.

The next morning when the cells were opened, the other prisoners came outside to find out about me. They were impressed that I had been accused in nineteen bomb blast cases and caught with an English weapon. They would not have believed that all the cases were totally false and I could not distinguish between a Wembly revolver and a pistol.

Tihar was the model jail created by Kiran Bedi. I had heard a lot about the langar or kitchen where the meals for all the jails were cooked. There was a convict called Dinoo; he was a Hindu but he joined the Muslims in offering namaaz and even kept the rozas.[6] He arranged a visit to the langar for me.

When I entered the huge kitchen, the first thing I

noticed was the strange silence and discipline. These were all convicts.[7] They had solemn expressions and no one smiled. All of them were occupied with different tasks in a hot and suffocating atmosphere.

I had never before seen such huge karhais (woks). They were so big that it needed five or six able-bodied men to carry one wok and lift it to put it on the gas stoves. The convicts told me that before the gas stoves were introduced they had to cook on wood and charcoal stoves in which the flames could not be controlled easily and the danger of getting burnt was ever present.

I saw men kneading the atta in huge bowls and their knuckles bled and the blood got mixed with the atta. There was a huge table where men stood in a line to make rotis. One made a ball and the other flattened it and then a third person put it on a massive iron tawa or griddle. One man had the job of turning the roti and when it was done he threw it on a wire mesh above the fire. They had to make rotis for 2,500 prisoners and each prisoner had five rotis in each meal. So these men made 25,000 rotis every single day. Now I realized why so many rotis were burnt and some were not quite cooked.

I could not bear to stand for more than a few minutes there—it was so hot. These convicts did this work day in and day out. We undertrial prisoners got to go to the courts, meet family members and lawyers but these people rarely got visitors and some of them had got life imprisonment.

They worked hard in the hope that they would get three months' remission for each year. They were paid some paltry amount but many saved their money so they could support their families from the jail. Ravi, who was on death row, told me he wanted to work so he could earn because he wanted to send money to his family. But the death row prisoners are not allowed to work.

After I was convicted in one case I wanted to work so I could earn money and help with the legal expenses. But the jail authorities denied me permission.

On the way out I had to pass the ward where an elderly man was sitting and reading the Quran. His name was Qureshi Saheb but everyone called him Babaji or Chachaji. He was from Mumbai. His crime, to which he had pleaded guilty, was that he had tried to kill some people involved in the demolition of the Babri Masjid.[8] He had told the court that if he got out he would try again.

He called me and asked me to sit beside him. He talked to me and gave me advice. I wondered whether he had really tried to kill anyone or had he admitted to a crime he only imagined doing. He was not really of sound mind any more.

In the TADA vehicle I met a prisoner whose name was Shahbuddin Ghauri.[9] He had been a student of the Jawaharlal Nehru University and was in the jail in connection with the Hawala scam. He suggested that I enrol myself in IGNOU (Indira Gandhi National Open University). He also told me that there is a library where I could get books. He advised me to use my time in Tihar Jail to study and get a degree.

I asked the Head Warden about IGNOU but he told me that the procedure for admission was complicated; besides I would need special permission to go to the ward.

One day I managed to go into Ward No. 7 which was called the IGNOU ward. I was really impressed by the atmosphere. It was so clean and the people looked much nicer. The barracks were also much tidier. Before I could find out anything more, the guard who was in charge of me caught up with me and led me outside.

I never thought of asking my lawyer to get me permission from the court to join IGNOU. In the courts my mind was occupied with the proceedings. Besides it would have meant more fees for the lawyer.

Anyway, I persisted, and finally some jail officials did help and I got myself enrolled as a student. They had a special course called BPP which I had to pass and then I could get admission into the BA course.

I still remember the day I first entered the library. There was a long table with chairs and it was the first time I saw prisoners sitting on chairs. We always had to squat on the ground; we were not entitled to sit even on a stool. Only officers sat on chairs. I took in the quiet atmosphere and then I sat on a chair. I suddenly felt this simple act of sitting on a chair had restored some of my dignity and self-respect. After I was released from jail, one of the first things I did was to buy four chairs so that I could sit with dignity and speak to my guests.

It was really wonderful to become a student and I have still preserved my IGNOU identity card. I went for my classes and visited the library. It was in the library that I met a fair and soft-spoken young man who was the same age as I was. He sat next to me and introduced himself as Shahid Azmi.[10] He said he was in for a case under TADA and he too was enrolled in IGNOU. He said he too had been kidnapped by the police and falsely implicated.

We used to have discussions. I asked him why so many Muslims and Sikhs were in the jail on the various provisions of the law. I saw Shahid writing applications for other prisoners. Often the prisoners who could not read or write had to pay Rs 500 for one simple application. Shahid helped them to save money and trouble.

There was a small group of four or five of us, including Shahid and me, who would pool in our money to help new prisoners. I remember on one occasion a man had been arrested with a large quantity of RDX. We had read about him in the papers and learnt he was now in Tihar.

We knew that he would not have basic things like soap, toothpaste and so we pooled in money and bought him the basic toiletries and went to see him at the Mulahiza jail for new prisoners. We got permission from the warden. On that occasion, I went with an Afghani prisoner. The man turned out to be from Mewat village and his language betrayed his rural roots. He was around fifty-five to sixty years old. When we asked him why he had been arrested he said they had found some two or three kilos of Iodex (well-known balm for pain). He had no idea what RDX was. We explained to him that the charge sheet would be filed in three months. He should try and get a good lawyer. We then gave him soap, toothbrush and toothpaste and left him.

In March 2001 I was transferred to a cell of Ward No. 8—the high-security ward where the prisoners accused of terrorism were housed. Now my movements were severely curtailed and I could not go around anywhere. Even before my transfer, the jail authorities had restricted my movements and curtailed my rights.

While I was in the high-risk ward or 'Highlight' as it is called in the jail I had to share my cell with another prisoner. There was a time when one Sikh man called Kulwinder Singh from Amritsar was put in my cell. He and his brother were both arrested under TADA but they did not want to stay together. Kulwinder's brother was in a different ward.

Kulwinder was of a very religious bent of mind. He got up early in the morning and did ardas. He kept his utensils and water pitcher separately and did not want me to touch his things. His elder brother had tobacco and would share food and even his plate. The elder brother had friends among all communities but Kulwinder had only a few.

Kulwinder carried a photograph of Bhindranwale and told me about Operation Bluestar.[11] He said the Indian army drove a tank through the most sacred part the Harminder Sahib Gurudwara. He told me about how the Punjab jails were full of people arrested under the TADA and many youth were killed in false encounters; sometimes these youth were killed even inside the jail or while being taken to the court.

Kulwinder showed me a photo of his wife. He was arrested just a day or two after his wedding.

When his mulaqaat came, he got lots of stuff. His mother used to bring desi ghee, turbans, kameez-pyjama and fruits. He shared the food with me. He had money in his account. He said the Sri Gurudwara Prabhandhak Committee (SGPC) looks after the Sikh prisoners.

I also met Kashmiri prisoners. Many of them had been framed like I had been. The Kashmiris were regularly arrested around 15 August and 26 January; often the men were picked up from Azadpur Mandi where they had come to sell their fruits. Then they were tortured and told to confess to some terrorist act, made to sign blank pieces of paper and then they landed up in jail.

The Kashmiris were soft-spoken and polite and I did not see them as fundamentalists. Nearly all of them were well educated and could speak English. I wondered why Indian Muslims did not have that much education. They liked to read and were good with their hands. They could draw well or make roses with paper or darn clothes.

The Kashmiris really hated the food and longed for non-vegetarian dishes. Kiran Bedi had banned meat from the jail diet and even disallowed any family from bringing it. Many of the Kashmiri prisoners killed and roasted pigeons secretly.

The summer months were really bad for the Kashmiris. They would get prickly heat and feel very uncomfortable. The Kashmiri prisoners did not have visitors during the summer months—because of the heat no one wanted to come to Delhi. But from October they would get visitors and then I got an opportunity to taste Kashmiri food. It was delicious. I remember the paneer cooked in tomato gravy, lotus stems and their spicy walnut chutney. The Kashmiris did not particularly like the food from my home so I gave them fruits which they had never eaten such as custard apples and chikoo and litchis.

The Kashmiris were warm and generous. The only thing I did not like about them was that the moment they saw another Kashmiri, they would start speaking in Kashmiri and exclude me. Once I was with two Kashmiris in one cell. They spoke in their language even though I requested them to speak in Urdu. I felt very excluded.

Kashmiri Muslims looked down on Indian Muslims because we were poor and uneducated. They told me that the barbers in Kashmir are all UP or Bihar Muslims. They thought the Mumbai Muslims were better than the Delhi Muslims. They pitied us. But when I asked them whether they would welcome us in Kashmir, they would reply that it was not possible because they themselves were facing so many problems.

I used to see the Red Cross team visit the Kashmiri and Pakistani prisoners. I could not understand why these foreigners came to help them, especially Kashmiris whom I looked upon as fellow Indians.[12]

I wondered why no one came to meet us, the Indian prisoners. When the Red Cross team came I was thrown out of my cell so they could speak to the Kashmiris in private.

The Red Cross representatives sometimes brought their own doctor; how I wished I could have consulted him. And more than anything else I wished they would visit my family as they did the Kashmiri families. The Red Cross used to help to put pressure on both the jail authorities and convicts to treat the Kashmiri prisoners with respect.[13] But often there were brutal attacks on the Kashmiris.

In the beginning when I was being taken in the TADA vehicle to the court, I would enjoy listening to the exchange between the Sikhs and the Kashmiris. The Sikhs boasted that they had killed their enemies but the Kashmiris only went for soft targets. The Kashmiris retorted that the Sikhs had a lot of resources and had taken refuge in the US and Canada; the Sikhs said they had carried out their movement on a flat terrain whereas the Kashmiris had such high mountains to protect them. It was all said in a light vein but I felt uncomfortable in these kinds of discussion.

I remember in 1999 some leaders of the Hurriyat were transferred from the Jodhpur jail to Tihar Jail. I did not meet them but another prisoner called Ahmed who had stayed with them told me that they were not united and did not even eat together. I still remember Ahmed's comment: if the Kashmiri leaders could not share plates how would they solve the Kashmir problem. Ahmed had been with Charles Sobhraj.[14]

Then we got the shocking news that our Parliament had been attacked in broad daylight. I was shocked and shaken. The news spread throughout the jail like a wild fire. The four people accused of conspiring to attack the Parliament were arrested and brought to Tihar Jail.

Suddenly, the attitude of the Warden, the Head Warden and Tamil Nadu Special Police all changed. They started looking at all the Muslim prisoners as one; as if we were all equally involved or complicit in the attack.

The jail authorities began regular and more vigorous searches of the cells; but in the name of searching they just wanted to humiliate us. For instance, they would take a packet of detergent bought from the jail canteen and tear it so that all the soap lay scattered. Or pour the hair oil from the bottle on the pretext of looking for some contraband item.

They also said we could not buy any food or drink from the canteen; we were allowed to visit only the dry canteen. From now on we could not even have a cup of tea.

I was really shocked by the attack on our Parliament,

but I was also shocked by the way all of us Muslims had come under attack. I had never taken interest in politics but now questions came to my mind about the future of Muslims living in India. Would we always be looked upon with suspicion?

I saw so many Muslim young men being thrown into the jail. Many of these youth were members of SIMI.[15] I had never heard of the organization. I met Abdul Aziz, one of the senior leaders of SIMI. He was very quiet and well behaved.

I did not hear any of the SIMI members talking of violence. From them I learnt more about the Babri Masjid demolition, about the growing violence against Muslim, the Srikrishna Report[16] and how Muslims are discriminated against when it comes to jobs in government service and why we are poor. Later I realized whatever he was saying was documented in the Sachar Report.[17] Abdul Aziz asked how any country could advance if the minorities are not given the same opportunities as the majority community.

On Eid, Hindus joined in our celebrations and SIMI members did not mind; and on Holi they greeted the Hindus but did not play with colours. I loved playing Holi and put colour on the officers but not on the SIMI men. But I did not put colour when a Hindu said he was not playing since there had been a death in his family.

When I listened to these Muslim leaders and heard political discussions, I felt my heart sinking. I somehow knew that I would be affected by the growing hostility towards Muslims. I could feel that the attitude of the judge in the court had changed. Once he had even noticed that Abbu had not come to court and offered kind words of condolence, but now it seemed his attitude towards me had hardened.

Despite all these changes I could not entirely give up hope that I would be able to prove my innocence one day.

NOTES

1. Jail meant for those who are between the ages of eighteen and twenty years.
2. This was a part of the 'reform' introduced by Kiran Bedi who called Tihar Jail an ashram much to the resentment of many Muslim prisoners, especially those from Kashmir.
3. The Terrorist and Disruptive Activities (Prevention) Act was passed in 1985 and allowed to lapse in 1995. However, those arrested and accused for offences under the Act continued to be tried under its provisions. At the time of Aamir's arrest the TADA had lapsed. Aamir was not put into the high-security ward till March 2000.
4. Kiran Bedi was the Inspector General of Prisons from 1993 to 1995 during which time she introduced reforms in Tihar which won her the Magsaysay Award in 1994.

5. Jaspal Bhatti (1955–2012), Indian television personality famous for his comedy shows entitled *Flop Show* and later for his films; he ran a training school for comedians called the Joke Factory.
6. This was a common practice in the jail in which many Hindu prisoners kept the rozas and sometimes Muslims kept the Navratri fasts with their Hindu friends in the jail. This has been reported in the press from time to time.
7. The jail authorities are not allowed to make the undertrial prisoners work; only those convicted and serving time after sentencing have to work.
8. The Babri Masjid was a seventeenth-century mosque in Ayodhya in UP. Right-wing Hindus claimed that it had been built on the site of the birthplace of Rama. While negotiations, cases in court and talks were going on, the Babri Masjid was demolished by members of the Vishwa Hindu Parishad on 6 December 1992 in the presence of senior BJP leaders. Many believe that the demolishment was a planned event. The Muslims all over India were shocked and it is a watershed that marks the beginning of the rise of militancy among the Muslim youth and heightened communal tensions.
9. Shahbuddin Ghauri's contribution in motivating young prisoners to continue their studies has been noted by many, including Kiran Bedi. He was upheld as a model prisoner and after his release he continues to do social work in his village in Rampur district.
10. Shahid Azmi was arrested during the violence in

Mumbai following the demolition of the Babri mosque in 1992. Subsequently, he crossed over into Pakistan-administered Kashmir, where he spent a brief period at a militant training camp, but soon returned. In December 1994, he was arrested under the TADA for an alleged conspiracy to assassinate Shiv Sena leader, Bal Thackeray. He was finally acquitted by the Supreme Court. He spent seven years in jail during which time he studied law and when he was released, he became a lawyer and took up cases of people wrongly accused of being terrorists. He was assassinated in 2012. A film has been made based on his life called *Shahid* in 2013.

11. Jarnail Singh Bhindranwale (1947–84) was a politico-religious leader who wanted the Sikhs to go back to the pure form of Sikhism; he took sanctuary in the Golden Temple which he fortified. Indira Gandhi launched Operation Bluestar in June 1984 in which the Indian army rolled tanks inside the temple; Bhindranwale was killed in the operation. The Sikhs' highest temporal authority, the Akal Takht, described him as a martyr of the Sikh Nation, but the Indian government viewed him as an extremist.
12. Aamir looks upon Kashmiris as Indians. The Red Cross visited them as the UN considered them as residents of a disputed territory.
13. Red Cross access to Kashmiri prisoners was curtailed and finally stopped in later years.
14. Charles Sobhraj is a celebrity serial murderer who was in Tihar Jail from 1976 to 1997.

15. The Students Islamic Movement of India (SIMI) was formed in Aligarh in April 1977; it was banned after the Parliament attack. In the 1990s, SIMI called for jihad and Caliphate as a response to growing Hindu nationalism which led to the demolishment of the Babri Masjid.
16. Justice B.N. Srikrishna Commission investigated into the violence against Muslims in Mumbai between December 1992 and January 1993. The report implicated the Shiv Sena and the police in the violence; the report traced the root cause of the violence to the Babri Masjid. The recommendations of the Commission have not been enforced despite repeated demands by Muslim organizations and secular groups.
17. 'The Social, Economic and Educational Status of the Muslim Community of India: A Report, Prime Minister's High Level Committee', November 2006. The Committee was headed by Justice Rajender Sachar.

7

CAGED PRISONERS

~

'It was really scary—the silence and the isolation. The only thing that reminded me how beautiful life could be was the sight of flowers growing outside our ward; and I could see a big jamun tree and a smaller guava tree.'

Ammi had started coming to the court and meeting me in the jail. It was so painful to see her worried face. She had lost weight and looked permanently tired.

There were six bomb blast cases pending against me; and then there was the main case in which I was supposed to have been arrested carrying a revolver.

There were times I would ask her to take a message to my lawyer as he could not come to the jail to meet me; but she found it difficult to understand the complex legal proceedings or to read my notes. One cousin did accompany Ammi to court or to the jail; but it was Alia who helped Ammi write down what the lawyer had said.

Alia had not forgotten me. Once, I had seen her sweet face at the Tis Hazari courts. It was during the proceedings of the case filed against me by the police constable after he attacked me inside the jail. That was the only case being heard in open court. Alia had brought some chocolate for me but when she shyly tried to give it to me she was rudely told she could not give anything to the prisoner.

Ammi told me that Alia came to see her regularly, especially after she got a job in a school near our home. Alia would read out my letters and then remind Ammi of the tasks which had to be done.

One day I wrote directly to Alia to thank her and

she promptly replied to my letter. But even just to imagine her writing it had made me feel better. The one source of comfort for me in those days was the thought of Alia. I had read and re-read her letter so many times. Each time I read it I could see her face before me, just like you see in the Hindi films. In fact, the letter had nothing personal. She was only reporting what Ammi told her to write.

Once Alia accompanied Ammi when she came to see me during Raksha Bandhan. That was the only day we could meet face-to-face, the only day I could feel the warmth of Ammi's embrace and her kiss on my forehead. Alia had said nothing. I told you ours was a very old-fashioned love. But her presence had filled with me with indescribable joy.

The court proceedings were continuing but the judge was distant and cold. On 23 April 2003 he read out his judgement in two bomb blast cases in which I was accused of having planted bombs in the Karol Bagh area on 26 October 1997.

I waited quietly for the sentence. In the bomb blast case of Ghaffar Market the judge sentenced me to ten years imprisonment; and in the bomb blast at the Roshan Di Kulfi, I was given life imprisonment.

The same judge who had acquitted me in twelve similar cases now found me guilty. What was different now? It is true that in both these cases the prosecution produced witnesses who swore that they had seen me at the site. My lawyer argued that they were interested witnesses because they were injured.

I feel the witnesses had given false testimonies not because there was any personal enmity but now there was a growing enmity between Hindus and Muslims and Muslim youth were suspect in their eyes. I do not know how that fact can be brought before the court but that is what I believe to be the real truth.

The judge also observed that I had failed to adduce any evidence to prove that I had thrown the packet given by Guptaji at the Wagah border. In none of the earlier cases had he ever made such an observation. If only my lawyer had produced Ammi as my defence witness...

I wanted to appeal but where was I going to get a lawyer to appear for me in the High Court? I knew their fees would be much more and Ammi had no way of arranging any money.

My fellow prisoners suggested that I ask for legal aid and told me that I have a right to ask for a lawyer of my choice. They suggested three names: D.C. Mathur, Rajeev Dhawan and Rajesh Mahajan. I wrote an application through the Legal Aid cell in the jail on 5 March 2004 and I got a reply on 24 March 2004. I then sent another application to the High Court asking for a speedy trial.

The person who helped me write these applications was John from Shillong. He helped me write my applications, get my appeals typed and helped me to contact the right lawyers. He helped many people.

John had been a manager in a bank in Old Delhi and had developed a taste for the Old Delhi food; he used to get shammi kebabs and sheermals from outside. Since he had been given duty at the deodhi he could eat in relative safety.

John was really a decent guy and it was because of his decency that he got into trouble. He had organized a loan and stood as guarantor. When the businessman did not pay back the money he landed in jail when he readily admitted his mistake. He got three years' imprisonment.

I cannot really explain but even during the worst of times I never gave up hope of being free and then looking after Ammi. She had begun to look weak and fragile.

My application was accepted and my appeal came up for hearing before Justice R.S. Sodhi and Justice P.K. Bhasin. My lawyer, Rajesh Mahajan, did not come to meet me in the jail so I had to send Ammi and my sister, Aapi, to Rajeshji so that they could explain the case to him and tell him the real story. Since the hearing in the High Court does not require the presence of the accused, I did not ever meet him and did not know how he had presented my case.

On 18 January 2006 Rajiv Mehra, the Additional Sessions Judge, gave his judgement in the main case against me. In that case there were twenty accused; five of the accused had been discharged already. As I said, they had been able to get lawyers right from the beginning. Some accused had got light sentences after plea bargaining.

This was the case in which the police said I had been arrested coming out of a mosque. If only my lawyer had put Ammi in the witness box, she could have told the court how I had disappeared and she could have shown the letter I had been made to write to her. It was on the basis of the letter that she handed the police all my documents.

But at the time the thought did not occur to me.

In that case I was sentenced to ten years' imprisonment. Now I would have to find a way to appeal to the High Court.

Later that year, in August, I got some good news. On that day, in August 2006 I was called to the deodhi. I was told to go to the warrant room. There I found a havaldar who smiled at me and told me to make arrangements for mithai because the High Court had acquitted me in the case in which I was awarded a life sentence.[1]

I was jubilant and tears of joy came to my eyes. I asked him for a copy of the judgement; he asked for money. I shared my joy with my fellow prisoners by ordering laddoos from the canteen.

My faith in the higher judiciary had been strengthened.

Of course I was happy but I knew there were many more hurdles to be crossed before I could hope to be free and able to look after Ammi. There was the case in which I was accused of planting a bomb in Baba Cinema in Sonepat in Haryana. The bomb had exploded at five-thirty in the evening on 28 December 1996. According to the prosecution I had disclosed this during my interrogation after I was arrested in February 1998.

The co-accused, one Mohammad Alam, had already been acquitted in September 2002 but my trial had not even begun. The case was pending in a court at Sonepat.

Finally, I was put on trial after the Chandigarh High Court[2] gave an order to the Sessions Court at Sonepat to conduct the trial speedily. The first day the judge asked me whether I had a lawyer. I replied I did not. I was lucky that a lawyer named S.K. Tyagi offered to take up my case. I told him I could not give him any fees but he said we could discuss the matter later on and he took my vakalatnama.

In accordance with the rules, I should have been transferred to the jail at Sonepat but instead I was taken by a vehicle for each court hearing from Tihar. I really enjoyed the long ride; it was an opportunity to see the outside world. For me, it was like going on an outing.

Finally, on 16 March 2006, the judge acquitted me. He held: 'Simply the disclosure statement of the accused is no use to the prosecution but the same is hit by Section 27 of the Indian Evidence Act. The prosecution has not been able to prove its case.'

In almost all the nineteen cases against me the prosecution produced the same public witnesses. The two main witnesses were Chander Bhan and Abdul Sattar. According to the police, Chander Bhan had accompanied them when they went to raid the factory where Shakeel printed his sheets in Pilkhua and there they found material used for making bombs.

Abdul Sattar was the landlord whose room was rented by Shakeel.

Both these witnesses came for each case and testified. They were produced as prosecution witnesses but they refused to give false testimony. Chander Bhan told the court each time that he had never been to Pilkhua; Abdul Sattar admitted he was Shakeel's landlord but refused to falsely testify that he had seen his tenant making bombs or ever seeing me there.

It is remarkable how these two witnesses and so many others refused to tell lies despite considerable police pressure. After I was released I pointed this fact to a journalist who had come to interview me. The journalist traced Chander Bhan and asked him how he had been cited as a prosecution witness.

Chander Bhan told the journalist that he used to run a tea stall in Chandni Chowk when an acquaintance requested him to accompany him to the Chanakyapuri police station. At the police station he was made to sign a blank piece of paper. The next thing he knew he was summoned to court. In court he was asked by a lawyer whether he had witnessed the recovery of any explosives but Chander Bhan said he had never been to Pilkhua.[3]

Even though I was acquitted in the Sonepat bomb blast case, I still had three more cases pending against me in which trials had not even begun. Despite the fact that I repeatedly brought this to the notice of the jail authorities they took no steps to expedite the proceedings.

I decided to write directly to the Allahabad High Court and bring it to the notice of the court that a case against me was pending since 1997. My petition was read by Barkat Ali Zaidi, a judge of the Allahabad High Court and on 26 February 2007 he directed the district judge to proceed with the trial on a day-to-day basis and to personally monitor the progress of the case and keep the High Court informed. By now I had learnt quite a bit about the criminal justice system!

Finally in April 2007, I was transferred to Dasna Jail in Ghaziabad.

Dasna Jail was a fairly new jail and it was the first time I was seeing a double-storeyed one. It was evening when I entered. I saw all the prisoners were eating at the 'chakkar', except that it was called 'ghunti' in Ghaziabad. The nambardars wore flaming orange uniforms with red caps. The munshis below them wore white. I was told here in this jail I must never walk in the middle while going from the deodhi to the chakkar because only officers walked in the middle. I must walk either on the right or left side.

While going through the formalities I learnt that Shakeel was already lodged in Dasna. I was keen to meet him because he could help me in settling down in the new jail. When I was asked under what sections I was being charged, I mentioned the sections of the Indian Penal Code such as murder and grievous hurt but I did not mention the sections relating to the Explosive Substances Act. The reason was that I did not want to be sent to the high-risk ward or be isolated from the other prisoners. Also, I would face less prejudice and suspicion.

I had some experience of how to talk to officers and nambardars. I spoke politely with my hands clasped in front of me. I answered the questions quickly and without hesitation. I was much more confident now when I was confronted with the jail officials.

I also knew jail etiquette and understood how to handle the hierarchy. I found out that the nambardar who took charge of me had been in jail for just five years whereas I had been in Tihar Jail for ten years. That made me his senior.

I was sent to the Mulahiza jail for new prisoners. I picked up my thali and took the dal and sabzi. The food was even worse than it was in Tihar. I had never thought that there would come a day when I would actually miss the Tihar Jail food!

In the morning I was told to pick up a broom and start cleaning the barrack and sweeping the grounds. I refused. I said as an undertrial prisoner I was not required to do this kind of work. I knew my rights by now but it seemed the munshi had no idea about these rules.

While in Tihar Jail, I had read several books on human rights and the law in Hindi. When Abbu was alive he had bought me books on the Criminal Code and the Constitution of India. Now my knowledge was proving useful!

The other prisoners told me '*500 rupees ki ginti katni paregi*'—in other words, that I would have to give a bribe of Rs 500 to not work.

I was taken to the Deputy Jailor, Vikram Singh. He asked '*Tu safai nahi karega?*' I said I would keep my own area clean but I would not do anything against the law. He said: '*Vakil ban gaya hain! Yeh UP hai gitni katwane hote hain.*' (You want to be an advocate! This is Uttar Pradesh and here you have to give the bribe.) Despite his implied threat I stood my ground and earned respect from my fellow prisoners who started calling me Khan Saheb.

My life in Dasna Jail became much easier because of Aqil. Aqil had been sentenced to life imprisonment. He too had been transferred from Tihar Jail and he remembered seeing me there. I whispered to him not to mention that I was an accused in a bomb blast case. Aqil had influence in the jail and he took me under his wing. He introduced me to Kulbhushan Rawal who was educated and I consulted him about my cases.

I enjoyed being in the barrack with lots of different kinds of people. In the high-risk jail the men had only talked politics; I was fed up with them. I could not understand their talk on political issues and their seeming lack of concern with personal matters. I was worried about my mother's failing health and longed to see my father's grave—and they wanted to reform the world.

Here in the barrack, I learnt about the outside world from the prisoners. Someone told me about a thing called the Internet from which it was possible to access knowledge about the entire world. I also heard about mobile phones. In Tihar Jail I had heard that gang leaders had mobiles but I had never seen one close at hand. One of the criminals offered his mobile to me to speak to Ammi. It was really tempting but then I knew Ammi would get scared if she suddenly got my call; and if I was caught I would have yet another case on me. I had to guard my reputation. Then I was amazed to see so many channels on the television. When I was at home we had only Doordarshan. The world outside had changed so much.

I visited the library and there I met Vijay Singh, the convict in charge of the library. He had murdered someone in anger. Otherwise he was calm and a very knowledgeable man. I learnt yoga from him and we even got it introduced in the jail. He did not talk to most people. He was disciplined and really respected rules and regulations. The jail authorities relied on him.

Vijay Singh was called Babaji. He told me that the IGNOU had opened a centre in Dasna and I could enrol. I was really happy and once again picked up my studies. In Tihar I had managed to finish the school certificate so this time I was admitted into the BA course.

We used to be taken to the library and shown movies. I remember some of the movies. I enjoyed *Peepli Live*, which exposed the way the media behaves and I remember enjoying *Tere Bin Laden*. We also saw movies on cable TV.

The best part of the day in Dasna was when the munshi came to read out the list of people who were to be released. We would all gather around even when we knew our name was not likely to be called. I had never seen this in Tihar. The nambardar called out from the 'Rihai' list. Everyone gathered around him. It was just wonderful to see the expressions of the people who were being released. I think all of us would secretly imagine what it would be like to be free again.

I finally met Shakeel in court. The court lock-up was really filthy with red spit on the walls and the latrines were choked. There was no clean water and the number of prisoners stuffed inside the lock-up were so many that we felt suffocated. Then there was a system by which the rich prisoners paid to get their case heard first so they could get back sooner.

We had to have our breakfast and lunch together before going to court. We were not given anything to eat or drink the whole day while we waited for our case. Once again I began to appreciate my experience of Tihar Jail.

It was in the court that I saw Shakeel's family for the first time. They had all come together— his brother, his wife and three children (two daughters aged sixteen and eighteen years and a twelve-year-old son). Shakeel said when he was picked up by the police, the boy had been a baby and now he was a young boy. The family members kept asking him: 'When will you come back home?'

I had noticed that when a prisoner first enters the jail he really looks forward to meeting his family members. They all have hope that he will return. But as the years go by they lose hope, debts pile up and life becomes harder for the family. They tell him about their problems and he begins to feel helpless. Now the visits from the family bring little solace and he feels more disturbed than comforted. That is what had happened to Shakeel. He felt helpless seeing that his daughter had reached a marriageable age but how could he get her a good groom?

In a way that is what was happening with me. Now that Ammi was alone she had no one to unburden herself. She would share her problems with me, and it broke my heart. I felt so helpless. I could see her condition was deteriorating; she walked with difficulty. She forgot things easily and she became hard of hearing. I did not want her to travel all the way to Ghaziabad but I needed a lawyer. Ghazi Saheb had got me acquitted in twelve cases. It was not a small feat. But he could not come to Ghaziabad.

I had heard of N.D. Pancholi from other prisoners. They said he was a kind man and he did not charge exorbitant fees. I asked Ammi to contact him.

Pancholiji was indeed a man full of compassion and he readily agreed to take up my case. But this time I faced another problem. The judge was determined not to conduct the trial quickly despite the order and direction of the Allahabad High Court.

Judge Umesh Chand Pande did not comply with the Allahabad High Court's orders; he delayed fixing the date for commencement of the trial. The prosecution had filed a list of forty-three witnesses and none had been produced so far.

Then there were many delays because of lawyers' strikes. The Bar Association passed frequent resolutions calling for strikes on the smallest pretext. Sometimes it was because a lawyer had died or it could be a fight between two lawyers; and then there were elections to the Bar Association. There were several long strikes by the lawyers in support of their demand for a Bench of the High Court in Meerut.

Kulbhushan and I decided to do something about the situation. He collected many facts and statistics about the delays and then we wrote a petition addressed to the President of the Bar Association. Many prisoners signed the petition and then we posted it. A local newspaper got to know of our campaign and carried a report on our grievances.

We followed up with more petitions demanding basic amenities such as drinking water and fans at the court lock-up; and we demanded that the lock-up and its surrounding area be cleaned properly.

Our interventions did lead to some reforms and even the practice of giving bribes to get a quick hearing in court was stopped. But then the criminals who had benefited from the previous arrangements were angry with us; we had to be careful when we made demands.

In November 2007, there were bomb blasts in Uttar Pradesh.[4] That was when the officers of the Local Intelligence Unit (LIU) started coming to meet me. One of them was Vijay Singh and he came in civil dress to the court and asked me whether I knew anything about the new bomb blasts and I told him I did not know anything about any bomb blasts. He threatened to frame me in the latest bomb blasts and I got really scared. He even asked Ammi some questions while she waited for my case to come up.

Vijay Singh said he would make sure that I was punished. This was not Delhi, here in UP they could do anything with me. That was his response to my telling him I had been already acquitted in fourteen cases.

The day Vijay Singh came to speak to me while I was in the court lock-up, I was not taken to the court. Instead the files were taken out of the courtroom and I was made to mark my presence while sitting inside the lock-up. And the next day the *Dainik Jagaran* carried a report that I was a Pakistani terrorist.

Kulbhushan advised me to put it on record that the LIU officer had threatened me. He also advised me that I should make another application to put on record that I was brought to court in handcuffs.

Kulbhushan said that by putting on record that I was being made to wear handcuffs, they could not kill me in a false encounter by saying I was running away.

As a result of the visits of LIU, the prison authorities got alerted to the fact that I had been booked for possessing explosives. They were angry with me for not telling them. And they took me away from the general ward and put me in the solitary cell of the high-risk ward which is called Tanhai Ucch Suraksha Ward (Solitary High Security Ward) but referred to as just Tanha (Alone) in short form.

Shakeel was already there; he and I were in different cells. It was even worse than Tihar Jail. We were kept locked inside our cells for twenty-two hours. We were allowed to go out for one hour in the morning, from 7 a.m. to 8 a.m.; and then one hour in the evening from 5 p.m. to 6 p.m. Even our meals were served inside the cell and the toilet was also in the cell.

It was really scary—the silence and the isolation. The only thing that reminded me how beautiful life could be was the sight of flowers growing outside our ward; and I could see a big jamun tree and a smaller guava tree. The first time I set my eyes on a guava tree was when Abbu took me to his village near Allahabad.

The District Judge kept postponing the proceedings in my trial. There were long gaps between one witness and the next. Even though the trial had begun it was going very slowly. Ammi had been admitted to hospital and my lawyer made an application in January 2009 for permission to visit her. But the judge refused. It was then that I felt there was discrimination against me because I was a Muslim. Attitudes had hardened and with it the officials had become dehumanized.

Now I could see the pattern in the discrimination. While I was still at Tihar Jail I had seen how the jail authorities treated the Shiv Sainiks with kid gloves when they were arrested for vandalizing the cricket pitch at Kotla to prevent a one-day international cricket match between India and Pakistan in 2005. They were treated like honoured guests, not criminals.

In contrast the members of the PAC who had committed murders of so many Muslims in the 1980s were roaming free and had not been punished.[5] They had murdered more than forty Muslim youth in broad daylight and dumped their bodies in the Ganga canal.

I had already been acquitted in fourteen bomb blast cases; it was obvious I had been framed. In any case I had been in jail for more than a decade and I was not allowed to visit my widowed mother who was seriously unwell.

I was denied bail. When Ammi's condition worsened I tried again for bail but it was rejected.

Shakeel was having his own share of sorrows. Both his daughters were reaching marriageable ages. He was worried about his family. He had been in jail for ten years; he wondered whether he would get old before he could be free. We consoled each other; after all we had been acquitted in so many cases. But the attitude of the judge had really made him depressed. He had lost hope.

I saw that four or five days before his death he had changed. He was much more irritable and did not speak so much and started strolling on his own. He did not talk to anyone, even to me. I would see him making hand gestures as if he was talking to himself. He was mentally stressed. The warden also noticed and he even asked me why he had become like this in the past three years when he was okay for ten years.

I remember it was a hot afternoon in June 2009. Shakeel and I were in our respective cells; he in Cell No. 5 and I in No. 8. In between there were two empty cells. It was around two or three in the afternoon and as usual, I had dozed off. Suddenly I was woken up by unusual noises. I could hear people talking. One convict passed in front of my cell and I asked him what happened. He told me that Shakeel had hanged himself.

My heart started beating so fast. I could see the jail

officers. The Head Warden asked me whether Shakeel had said something to me. There was an eerie silence. I could not see things clearly. When they were taking Shakeel's corpse I saw only his feet. The warden said they were taking him to the hospital. I hoped against hope he would survive.

That evening I was not allowed out of my cell even for that one hour. Officers came but they did not tell me he had died. I was told he was in hospital. But a nambardar told me that Shakeel had made a noose with his bedsheets and had hanged himself from the fan. He also told me that there was a piece of paper tied to his feet. I wanted to know what was written in the paper.

My blood pressure shot up and I had to be admitted to the hospital. All of us prisoners demanded that we be shown the paper tied to Shakeel's foot. It was a suicide note and Superintendent V.K. Singh showed it to us. Shakeel said he was committing suicide because the trial was taking so long and the attitude of the judge showed that he would not give justice.

The magistrate who made an inquiry did not want to expose the fact that Shakeel had been driven to committing suicide because of the judiciary; and so the blame for Shakeel's suicide was firmly put on the jail. Shakeel's brother also filed a case against the jail authorities. It was also said that the post-mortem report showed that Shakeel had been poisoned; but I do not believe that was true. I think it was a part of the cover-up and in the process Superintendent V.K. Singh got arrested on charges of murder.

Shakeel's death was widely reported in the newspapers. In the course of investigating that story one journalist, Mohammad Ali, who was working in *Two Circle Net* wrote a detailed story about me and how I had been framed. Then Aziz Burney Saheb of *Sahara* (Urdu) also wrote and the outside world heard my side of the story.

The District Judge was transferred; but the one who came in his place did not do any better. The proceedings were just not moving ahead. Then a third judge came and under his supervision the trial did speed up.

Meanwhile my exams came up in May 2011 and I was taken to the jail in Meerut where Gandhiji had also been imprisoned. That was the IGNOU exam centre and it was a relief to be away from Dasna. Around that time the warden of Dasna asked me to enter an inter-prison essay writing competition being organized on the occasion of Gandhi Jayanti. I thought what was the point of my writing about Gandhiji when I had been condemned as a terrorist? Who will believe that I am truly inspired by his ideals and I had read about him in the jail? I was finally persuaded by Kulbhushan to write the essay.

I was really surprised when I was told I had won the first prize. It was even published in *Karagar Bandi Jeevan* magazine in its April–June 2011 issue.

How did I survive those terrible days after Shakeel's suicide?

It was because of my beloved Alia. Now we wrote to each other regularly and the conduit was none other than my lawyer, Pancholiji. I wanted to send her a gift but what could I send to her from the jail? I plucked flowers which blossomed in the garden, especially the roses. I then dried the petals between the pages of my books. These flower petals were enclosed in my letters to Alia.

The judge hearing the case suggested to Pancholiji that Ammi should be produced as a defence witness. Pancholiji brought her in his car and gently pushed her into the court in a wheelchair. Ammi could barely speak but she told the judge about how I disappeared in February 1998. My first defence witness.

On 18 July 18 I was acquitted by Judge Sanjeev Yadav. In his judgment he gave the details of my story and I felt he had genuinely listened to the defence.

NOTES

1. *Mohd Amir Khan* [sic] *v State 138* (2007), *Delhi Law Times* 759 (DB). See Appendix I.
2. Chandigarh is the shared capital of both Punjab and Haryana.

3. Indrani Basu, '"Witnesses" who didn't cave in, gave Aamir freedom back', *Sunday Times*, 26 February 2012.
4. On 24 November 2007 there were almost near simultaneous explosions outside the lawyers' chambers in court complexes in Lucknow, Varanasi and Faizabad; it was suspected that the blasts were a reprisal against lawyers for refusing to defend men accused of terrorism.
5. The Provincial Armed Constabulary (PAC) committed a series of murders during the riots in Meerut in May 1987. The trials are still going on.

8

NATIONAL OUTRAGE

~

'It seemed that the Government was not going to help in my rehabilitation. I was not entitled to it...because I had been acquitted on grounds of "reasonable doubt". How many more legal tricks will they use to deprive me of my basic rights guaranteed under the Constitution of India?'

On 12 January 2012 I stepped out of Rohtak[1] jail a free man, after thirteen years and ten months in prison.

It all happened so suddenly, so unexpectedly.

One year before that date I had been transferred to Rohtak Jail. There were two cases of bomb blasts pending since 1997. On the first day I appeared in the Rohtak court, the judge asked me whether I had a lawyer. I told him I did not; and that I could not afford one. He sent me to the Legal Aid Cell.

It was at the Legal Aid office I met advocate Rajesh Sharma. I straightaway told him I had no money, not enough even for my mother's treatment. He said that was not an issue. And he never even asked for costs of filing the petitions.

In one case I was accused of planting a bomb in the New Vegetable Market in Rohtak on 22 February 1997. Nearly twelve years after the event I was tried and acquitted. Subhash Tandon appeared yet again as a prosecution witness in the hope of securing my conviction. But the judge found that there were 'various infirmities and discrepancies' in the prosecution's case and acquitted me on 26 February 2011.

Now there was just one other case pending against me. Even in those cases that I had been convicted, I had already served more time than the sentence required.

The trial was going on from March 2010. The judge noticed I had been declared a proclaimed offender even though I was in the custody of the police.

The prosecution witnesses had given their testimonies.

Rajesh was ready with his final arguments. But before he could begin the judge told him it would not be necessary. Then the judge bent his head and scribbled something in his file, after which he looked up and turned to me and told me that I was free. As simple as that.

I was taken back to the jail. I shared my news with my fellow prisoners. They were really happy for me and we celebrated the moment. I gave away my books and packed my bags. I had only Rs 250 in my account.

Then I felt scared. It was evening and no one was there to receive me. The key turned in the big lock, the door opened and I stepped out with a bag in my hand and took a deep breath. I turned left and then to the right. There were no guards. I had no handcuffs and I was truly free. I was alone but I was free. I looked up at the sky. I turned left and walked in that direction; I went back and turned to the right and walked in that direction. I was so thrilled I could walk in any direction and no one was there to tell me where to go. I wanted to feel my freedom. I turned back one last time to look at the gate of the jail and the tower and walls. I did not look back again.

Luckily for me the Rohtak jail at that time was right in the middle of the town and I had just to cross the road to reach the bus stand. But I felt scared crossing the road. For nearly fourteen years I had not crossed a road on my own. It was growing dark and I felt a growing sense of insecurity.

I managed to cross the road and reach the bus stand; then I asked for a STD booth from which I dialled my sister's telephone number. Aapi picked up the phone. She just would not believe that I was speaking to her; that I was free and coming home. She could not believe me. I told her I was at the bus stop. I wanted someone to know where I was; in case the police decided to kidnap me again. If I disappeared again my sister could testify that I had phoned from the bus stop at Rohtak.

I got on to the Haryana Roadways bus going to Delhi. I sat down and waited for the bus to start. I felt a growing anxiety that the jail authorities may come to get me again. I saw small children get into the bus and watched with fascination their small hands and feet. It felt odd sitting in the company of ladies.

The bus started off and I noticed the traffic and saw vendors coming to the bus windows to sell small packets of peanuts. It was dark and the street lights seemed to be so bright. I kept a sharp look-out for the police in case they suddenly pounced on me from somewhere. As we entered Delhi I was amazed at how brightly lit it was. I admired the broad roads and looked with awe at the crowds of people busily going in all directions. I noticed there were clocks on the traffic lights which told you how many minutes there were for the lights to change.[2] I saw a metro station and was amazed;[3] for the first time I saw huge buildings which I learnt later were shopping malls.

The bus stopped at the Inter-State Bus Terminal at Kashmiri Gate but with all the underbridges and flyovers I almost did not recognize where I was. I got an auto and asked him to take me to Old Delhi.

I arrived back in my neighbourhood. There were many more shops and it was much more crowded than I remembered. But much had also remained the same. The narrow lanes and uneven roads and the tangle of electrical wires were the same. I heard the azan for Isha ki namaaz. It was at this time, nearly fourteen years ago, I had left home for the night prayers; and after the namaaz I had not returned. Now I was returning but I felt like a stranger.

I paid off the auto and quickly climbed up to the third floor, the same house which I had left so suddenly. Ammi had been cooking for me. When I arrived upstairs my sister came rushing to embrace me and started crying. She had called up our relatives to share the news of my return; most were too scared to come but a few had turned up. They greeted me.

I saw that Ammi was lying on the bed. When she saw me she knew that I had come home. But she could not get up and she could not speak. I held her tightly and did not let go. I told her: '*Ammijan, main aa gaya*.' She had become so thin and her once plump cheeks had wasted away.

After everyone had gone I climbed up to the roof and sat there watching the stars. If only Abbu had been there.

I came back to Ammi. I looked around the room. She had kept all my belongings safely. She had refused to give away any of my things. I saw the tape recorder which I had bought—Ammi had not allowed my nephew to take it. She told him that her son would want it when he came back. She had never given up hope. Now her son had returned but she could not speak. Her stroke had taken away her power of speech; but not the light in her eyes with which she expressed her joy at seeing me.

On the first day that Abbu met me in jail he had given me a nasiyat;[4] and I remembered it throughout my time in jail. He told me that even in the jail I would find good, educated people and bad, uneducated people. I must never keep the company of the bad; seek out the educated and learn from them.

I had learnt many things from my fellow prisoners—from the skills of an engineer to Ayurvedic cures for simple diseases. I had been told that the sign of good health was a cool forehead and warm hands. Before my transfer out of Tihar and later from the Ghaziabad jail I had applied and got character certificates. The certificates were testimonies to my good character and exemplary conduct throughout my stay in the jail. I had not acquired any bad habits and I had preserved my integrity.

I had got the certificates by applying under the Right to Information Act. The RTI is the best gift for our generation. I was the first one to use it to get character certificates from Ghaziabad.

The reason I applied for these character certificates was because I had thought they would help when I applied for a job. And that they may even help me win the hand of my Alia who had waited for me for thirteen years and ten months.

The thought of Alia made me smile and I fell asleep. Tomorrow I would begin life as a free man.

My topmost priority was to look after Ammi. Before I went to prison she had done everything for me. Now I had to do everything for her. In prison I had learnt to wash clothes and clean my room but I did not know how to cook. So I could not cook a hot meal for her. I had to buy food from the bazar and feed Ammi. Of course my sister sent food whenever she could. But for her too it had been a strain looking after her small children and also Ammi.

I took Ammi to the hospital; I wanted to provide the best possible health care. It was not an easy job. I had to climb down three floors and arrange for a rickshaw then climb back upstairs and pick up Ammi and bring her down. Once we got out of our narrow lane I would transfer Ammi into an autorickshaw and take her to the hospital; and then when we returned I had to carry her upstairs. The day I took Ammi to the doctors I was exhausted. I had very little strength in my limbs.

I realized that my health had suffered considerably. Sometimes I heard a strange whistling noise in my left ear. It must have been the result of the resounding slaps I got on my ears. I also found I could not digest food cooked in too much oil and spices. I could not eat chillies. My eyes were weak and mentally it was difficult to adjust to life outside prison.

And yet there was no time to recover and get back my strength; I knew I had to find a job; there were Ammi's medical bills to be paid, then there were accumulated debts which had to be repaid and more urgently, our house needed repair. The walls had cracks and one day I discovered that the roof was leaking. Ammi had squeezed herself into a corner to avoid getting wet.

Another day when I came back I found the atta scattered all over the floor; the tawa on which chappatis were made was lying in one corner and the tongs in another. I wondered what had happened till I saw that Ammi's hands were full of atta. I understood that my mother had tried to get up and make rotis for me. She had been feeling terrible that she could not cook. I hugged her and told her never to try that again. It was my turn to look after her.

I knew I must find a job quickly. Even before I could get one I needed an identity card for myself. All my certificates and my passport were still lying in the court. I found a ration card in which my date of birth was given as 1981. On the basis of that ration card I managed to have my Aadhar card made and then a Pan card.

The real struggle would be to get people to accept me; even now few had the courage to talk to me. Friends and neighbours avoided me. It was the Urdu press which came to my rescue. My story had already been published by Mohammad Ali of *Two Circles Net.*[5] But it was when *Sahara Urdu* serialized my story that there was a breakthrough. Aziz Burney Saheb[6] himself visited my home.

The newspapers and later the television channels carried pictures of me sitting with Ammi. People's perceptions started to change slowly; even the way they looked at me changed. The mohallawale, the people of the neighbourhood, started talking to me;

shopkeepers and old friends no longer avoided me. Now the neighbours greeted me and felt proud that our defamed neighbourhood had proved it was not a base for terrorism. From being portrayed as a dangerous terrorist, I was being looked upon as a victim of a system which discriminated against Muslims.

One evening a constable and a havaldar knocked at my door. It was the first time anyone in khaki uniform had come to our home after my release. They were carrying a wireless set. Ammi saw the uniformed men and her face immediately expressed her fear.

I went into the house and brought out my character certificates; they saw it and said it was good. Then they told me that they had been sent to tell me to report to the Secretariat and meet a senior bureaucrat, Arvind Ray. Then I went to the Bara Hindu Rao police station and met the station house in-charge, Pankaj Sharma. I requested him not to send the police to my house, especially in uniform. If they needed to talk to me they could ask me to go down to the police station.

The next day I met the senior bureaucrat, Arvind Ray, at the Delhi Secretariat. He said he had heard about my case and the Delhi government would help in my rehabilitation. He asked what I wanted and I replied that I would like a job, treatment for Ammi and a house. He listened to me and said something would be done. My hopes were raised and I waited for a response.

But as time went by I got no further news. Because of the publicity I received in the media, several political parties like the Communist Party of India (Marxist) and the Lok Jan Shakti also took up my cause; they included my case in the list of Muslim youth who had been wrongly arrested and detained. The parties wrote petitions to demand that all of us be given rehabilitation. They sent their petitions to Delhi's Chief Minister, Sheila Dixit, and even to the President of India. I accompanied them when they submitted their petitions. But nothing came of these meetings.

After I came back from prison, I had wanted to meet my lawyers and thank them. I first went to meet Feroze Khan Ghazi with a box of sweets. He was very warm and he told me many stories about how Abbu had struggled during those days. Ghazi Saheb was involved in work within the community as well as in the Lawyers for Minorities in South Asia. He said he would think about an appropriate job for me.

Next I went to meet Pancholiji and he was also warm and welcoming. I met all the lawyers except my lawyer in Sonepat because I was not comfortable travelling long distances on my own. The lawyers were surprised that I had remembered them.

Finally, it was Feroze Khan Ghazi Saheb who suggested I contact Shabnam Hashmi[7] who was deeply involved in working for democracy and secularism. I went for a meeting organized by her organization, called Anhad. The meeting was held at Delhi's Constitution Club. There I heard issues being raised which were dear to my heart and I heard many victims like myself speak about how Muslims are discriminated against and denied their fundamental rights.

There was an exhibition of posters which I liked and most of all I liked the fact that Hindus, Muslims and Christians had come together on one platform. I enjoyed listening to the songs which were inspiring; and speeches of political leaders such as Digvijaya Singh of the Congress Party and Brinda Karat of the Communist Party of India (Marxist). It was at that meeting I heard passionate speeches by people like Ram Punyani[8] and Mahesh Bhatt, the film-maker.

I started getting job offers from some individuals as well as from Islamic religious organizations. These religious organizations only came to help me once my case was given publicity by the media. I was angry that they had not helped me all these years. I was especially angry that none of them had helped my parents. If they had supported my family then perhaps Abbu would have been alive and Ammi may not have got a stroke.

The first person who nominated me for an award was Lenin Raghuvanshi, a founding member of the People's Vigilance Committee on Human Rights (PVCHR). PVCHR gave me the Jan Mitra Award and also gave me Rs 60,000 at a ceremony in July 2012 at which the Chairman of the Human Rights Commission was present. Apart from the fact that I needed the money, the fact that I was being recognized as a survivor, a human being who had suffered so much and yet had come out of it without losing my humanity, went a long way towards making me feel a part of society again.

But it is also true that religious organizations gave me financial help; and they gave it quietly. Jammat-i-Islam and Jammat-Ulama-Hind (Arshad Madni group) both gave me enough money with which I could buy a new house on the first floor. I wanted it to be big enough so I could provide Alia a good home. I was determined to marry Alia and give her a comfortable life.

Many individuals also gave me money and helped in many different ways. I was even presented an air conditioner, but did not have money to pay the electricity bill.

I finally decided to work with Anhad.

When I began I did not know how to even start a computer; so that was my first task. I learnt to e-mail and used my contacts with the media to mobilize it for Anhad's programmes. I also had experience with courts and lawyers so I helped people who came with their cases to Anhad.

I also learnt to mobilize students from colleges for our meetings and later when I worked in Muzaffarnagar with the victims of riots, I would take these students as volunteers. The Muslim victims had been stunned by the vicious communal violence let loose on their community by the miscreant Jats. It was a shock because even during the days before the Partition of India this area had remained peaceful and no one from this area had migrated to Pakistan.

I wanted the victims to see that there were many Hindus, Sikhs and Christians who were not communal. I organized the relief work and brought blankets, medicines, food and toys for the kids. I also helped Siyasat[9] set up their computer schools. I was also involved in a school in Old Delhi which had been set up by the Tammir-e-Millat Foundation.

Now I had a job and a new house on the first floor with two rooms and a balcony. I chose it because I can see the sky from the windows and the balcony. I get air and sun.

Dr Mohsin Wali at the Ram Manohar Lohia Hospital was looking after Ammi. He had been the physician to the President of India and under her care she had improved but still could neither walk nor speak.

It was a time to formally ask Alia's father for his daughter's hand. Normally an elder from the family should go with the proposal but I had no one so I went myself and asked him. I was not scared. After all I had learnt to talk to the police and jail authorities—talking to my future father-in-law could not be anything like talking to the superintendent of prisons!

Alia's father refused. He said it may be true that I had been acquitted but how could he marry his daughter to a man who had spent fourteen years in a prison. What would people say?

Alia and I considered running away and getting married in a court but we thought it would not be nice. So I came up with an idea. I led a delegation of people to her father consisting of all the respectable men from our community, including my lawyer Feroze Khan Ghazi, a doctor, a chartered accountant, businessmen who had helped our family including Chawla Saheb's son, and arrived at Alia's father's doorstep. The delegation put forward the proposal. Finally Alia's parents agreed.

On 12 October 2012, Alia and I got married. Her father had the nikah in a banquet hall in the Town Hall. I organized our walima in a haveli in Azad Market. I invited everyone I knew. Of course all the relatives came but more than our relatives was my new circle of friends and well-wishers.

I sent the wedding cards to all my lawyers; Pancholi Saheb's name was printed on the wedding card as my guardian. On the morning of my wedding I got a phone call from Mahesh Bhatt congratulating me and wishing me well.

I had not expected so many people to respond to my invitation. I was delighted to see that Lenin Raghuvanshi came all the way from Benaras. My lawyers were all present except Rajesh Sharma; but he sent his father with a present for me. Dr Wali came as did the SHO of Bara Hindu Rao police station, not as a policeman but as honoured guest.

Many journalists attended my reception, including Aziz Burney, the BBC correspondent Iqbal Ahmed, Mohammad Ali from TCN and Manoj Mitta; political leaders and MPs like Adeeb Sahib,[10] Asif Mohammad Khan, the Member of the Legislative Assembly (MLA) of Delhi elected from Okhla, and Ram Vilas Paswan[11] were all there. Some people turned up even though I did not personally invite them, like Arundhati Roy the writer. I wish I could name all my guests because the presence of each one was an act of solidarity.

I had organized a buffet. I had arranged for both vegetarian and non-vegetarian food. I found those who were supposed to eat non-vegetarian also took the vegetarian food. There was chicken biryani, korma and aloo salaan, kheer and cold drinks. It was typical Old Delhi fare and I could see everyone really enjoyed the dinner.

The best part of our wedding was to see Ammi sitting in a wheelchair smiling. The SHO came to congratulate her. The relatives and neighbours were amazed to see my distinguished guests. How I wished Abbu was there to see this moment. I am sure he would have been proud of his son.

Abbu's friends and others helped me meet the wedding expenses and we had a little left for our honeymoon. Alia and I went to Kulu and Manali and tried to put the past behind us. I even managed to go paragliding. I had lost my fear. At least the time in jail had made me a braver person.

We returned to our new home but found that the past cannot just be left behind.

Journalists came to interview me and sometimes I would relate how I was tortured. When they left I would find that Alia had been listening and her eyes would be red with crying. She would ask me about my days in jail but I did not want to burden her with those experiences.

At night she would wake me up looking very frightened. When I asked what had happened she would tell me I was crying out in pain. I told her that I get nightmares and she should not worry but just wake me up. Although I enjoyed my work I had to take many buses and by the time I got back I was tired and then I was irritable and got angry for apparently no reason.

My appeals were still pending in the High Court; although I could not be sent to jail even if the appeals went against me, I did not want the stigma of being convicted in any terrorist-related case. And the police were still after me.

One day I was called to the CBI Headquarters because the police wanted me to confront Tunda.[12] Pancholiji agreed to accompany me. I was produced before the man they said was Tunda, responsible for forty bomb blasts.

He turned out to be quite an old man. The police asked him whether he knew me. My heart was thumping; after all, this could be another ploy to frame me. But the man said no, he had never seen me. Then I was asked whether I had seen him before. And I, of course, said I had not.

Then in 2014, a case against me came up before the Special Director (Appeals) FEMA.[13] Once again Pancholiji came with me. From what I could understand, since it was in a mixture of Hindi and English, the judge was convinced that I was not guilty and should not have been fined Rs 50,000. However, he felt some compulsion to find me guilty despite the lack of evidence and I had to pay a fine of Rs 5,000.

This is the order passed by Shri Durga Charan Dass, Special Director (Appeals) FEMA:

> The appellant at the age of 18 was sent to jail in 1998 and released from jail in 2012, after 14 years. He had been acquitted by the District Sessions Court in 17 cases out of 19 cases. The Show cause notice by the Adjudicating Authority was not properly served on him. He was sent to his house address, while he was in jail. Thus considering all the facts and circumstances of the case, I take a lenient view and restrict the penalty imposed by the Adjudicating Authority to Rs.5000/- from Rs.50000/- through [sic] the department could not prove the possession of US $ 1200 from appellant.
>
> Sd/- Special Director. 11.06.2014

I borrowed the Rs 5000 from Pancholiji and paid the fine.

It seemed that the government was not going to help in my rehabilitation. There was no official response but I found out why I was not being given any compensation by accident when I was invited to participate in a programme on NDTV with Barkha Dutt. It was called *The Buck Stops Here*. Barkha asked a senior police officer, also invited to the programme, why I had not been given rehabilitation and the police officer replied that I was not entitled to it because I had been acquitted on grounds of 'reasonable doubt'. How many more legal tricks will they use to deprive me of my basic rights guaranteed under the Constitution of India?

Anusha came into our lives on 9 March 2014. Now our lives revolve around our beautiful baby. But then the thought crosses my mind—what does the future hold for Anusha Khan? I want to give her a really good education. I wish I could have finished my studies but the jail authorities did not allow me to attend the IGNOU after I was put into the high-risk cell.

I want Anusha to study. I would like her to devote her life to fighting against injustice and her education should help her understand the world around her. I have not been able to do formal studies but the years in jail have been an education. I read the Bible, the Ramayan and the Gita in the jail; unfortunately I could not get Guru Granth Sahib. I also read the Quran in translation. It is my feeling all these religions were like a Constitution at a given historical time. They are like rivers which all join the sea. I respect all religions.

Perhaps what I can teach my daughter is the art of positive thinking. It was my ability to think positively that helped me survive; and helped me keep alive the ray of hope that one day I would be free. Later, I got a Hindi translation of *The Amazing Results of Positive Thinking* by Norman Vincent Peale. I realized that I had an inborn capacity to remain positive.

Of course, it is for Anusha to decide what she wants to do with her life. I can only advise and guide; so much depends on the political atmosphere of the time. That will be the deciding factor for her future.

I still live with fear because the situation in our country is not good. Many Muslim youth are targeted and picked up by the police and I still feel vulnerable. There are still two appeals pending in the High Court and I hope I will be acquitted. Sometimes I do wish I could leave India, my country, and settle somewhere safe. But then I wonder where that place is?

NOTES

1. Rohtak is in Haryana some 84 kilometres from the Inter-State Bus Terminal in Delhi
2. Aamir is referring to the Traffic Signal Countdown Timers.
3. The Delhi Metro Railway Corp was created on 3 May 1995 as a part of the urban mass rapid transportation system; the first metro was inaugurated in 2002.
4. Advice given usually by elders.
5. Massachusetts-based e-journal; the two circles symbolizing India and the Muslim world. Mohammad Ali now works for *The Hindu*.

6. Aziz Burney was Group Editor of *Roznama Rashtriya Sahara* (daily), *Bazm-e-Sahara* (Monthly) and *Aalmi Sahara* (weekly); he left the Sahara group and started his own Urdu paper *Aziz-ul-Hindi* in 2013. He energized Urdu journalism but has been criticized for sensationalism.
7. Shabnam Hashmi started an organization called Act Now for Harmony and Democracy (ANHAD) in March 2003 in response to the carnage of Muslims in Gujarat in 2003. Her brother, Safdar Hashmi, was a theatre person and was murdered by goons while performing a street play for workers.
8. Ram Punyani was a professor of biomedical engineering at the IIT at Mumbai but he took early retirement to work full time for communal harmony.
9. Hyderabad-based media house which brings out an Urdu daily and has set up computer centres for the youth of the Old City.
10. Mohammad Adeeb, Member of the Rajya Sabha, who had launched a nationwide campaign against the arbitrary arrests of Muslim youth; he was against Muslims forming their own political parties. Instead he thought they should fight against communalism inside all parties.
11. Born in a Scheduled Caste family, Ram Vilas from Bihar opposed the Emergency imposed by Indira Gandhi and was in jail; he started the Lok Shakti Party and has been a Union Minister.
12. It was reported in the newspapers that Tunda was

arrested in August 2013.There were many controversies over his arrest. In 2000 it was revealed that he died in Bangladesh, but later it was proved wrong. In 2006, he was arrested in Kenya, but later fled. He was carrying a Pakistani Passport No. AC 4413161 issued on 23 January 2013 in the name of Abdul Quddus.

13. Foreign Exchange Management Act, 1999.

ACKNOWLEDGEMENTS

I have received much kindness and help from many people and so I could say thank you for ever. Most of the people who helped me have already been mentioned in the book and many others know that I will always remember their acts of kindness and love even if I may have forgotten to mention their names.

I would like to gratefully remember my companions inside the various jails who helped me in so many ways: from drafting my appeals to smuggling food while I was in the Kasoori and to those who were by my side in the worst of times and kept up my spirits. Many of them are still behind bars; and they know that this is as much their story as it is mine.

I have been lucky that my lawyers have so sincerely worked for my release; and the witnesses who refused to give false witness; and to those judges who were fair.

I want to thank the people who have supported me after my release: the journalists and the political leaders from across the political spectrum who have extended their help and continue to do so. Because of their help I have been able to have faith in the possibility of all of us— Hindu, Muslim, Christian and Sikh—being able to feel an equal sense of belonging to our country.

I would like to especially thank Shabnam Hashmi and the team at ANHAD. It is now a second family to me. And Harsh Mander for extending his hand in solidarity.

My thanks to Nandita Haksar for persuading me to write my story and putting it in a political and legal context; and to Dr Achal Bhagat for taking me as his patient without any fees.

I would also like to thank Ravi Singh for so enthusiastically agreeing to publish my story and Paromita Mohanchandra for editing the book and patiently reading it out to me.

I am ever grateful to my family who had complete faith in me and worked tirelessly for my release. My sisters and brothers in law for their support, and specially Ammi who showed remarkable courage when she left the security of her home and came out in the world to fight for justice for her son. And Alia—for never giving up, for waiting for me and, above all, for my little Anusha, the source of delight and joy in my life.

Mornings with Ammi in our new home before leaving for office

Our last Eid together with Ammi, she passed away in the same chair a few days later

Alia and I on our wedding day

Alia is now my wife

Alia, Anusha and I at a seminar organized by Anhad

Anusha and I at a seminar on Human Rights

The electronic media describes me as a
mere victim of the system

I am speaking at a meeting organized by
Muslim leaders

AFTERWORD

It is October 2015 and Aamir and I are sitting together in my house in Delhi. He has read through the entire manuscript, sometimes asking for the meaning of a word or phrase. He is excited that his book will soon be published.

We are discussing the possible appendices for his book. He has brought his photos in a pen drive. The photographs are neatly arranged in folders; photographs of him speaking at various public meetings, news clippings of articles published on him, including a long article in the *New York Times*; photos of Aamir participating in protests and meetings and then a folder with his wedding photographs and another of his honeymoon in Manali.

I open the folder with his honeymoon photos. There are a series of photographs of Aamir paragliding. In the first one Aamir is just a speck in the sky and in the next there is a glider and then there is a picture of Aamir emerging from the skies in the paraglider and landing on the earth.

'I felt really free.'

'Did Alia not try the paraglider?'

'No, she was afraid.'

What does it feel like to be free? It is now almost four years since you walked out of jail?'

'Of course, I am free in a sense. I have all the basic amenities which I did not have in the jail. I can go where I want, meet whom I like and eat whatever I like. But I don't feel truly free.'

'Why do you say that?'

'My cases are still pending in the court. The High Court has still not heard two appeals. I do not know how many more years I have to wait to get justice.'

What about the National Human Rights Commission?

The National Human Rights Commission had issued notice in March 2014 directing the Delhi Police Commissioner to give a detailed report on the cases against Aamir. Now he has got news that NHRC has announced its intention of awarding five lakh rupees to him for fourteen years of wrongful confinement. But, he says, no amount can bring back what he lost in those years.

'What about your job? I heard you have left Anhad.'

Aamir says he has not left Anhad. He is still working there on a voluntary basis but their funds have dried up. He tells me that all the NGOs working on issues relating to peace, democracy, secularism and communal harmony are being targeted. He says the government is filing false cases against them. Aamir says Alia wants him to do some business and earn money. She is worried about their daughter because they both want to give her a good education. I remind him that I have also been advising him to do business; he could always do social activism in his spare time. He smiles uncertainly.

'Yes, I remember. I did try doing business.'

He says he put in Rs 50,000 of his money and started an artificial jewellery business with a partner. They made a profit of Rs 12,000 but the partner did not tell Aamir where he got the jewellery. Besides, Aamir says, most of the jewellery is available online. Why couldn't he also do online business? He said he needed some training. 'I have just started understanding the world. It will take me time.' He smiles.

The expression in his eyes does not match the brightness of his smile. 'Do you still get nightmares?' I ask.

'No. I am much better. But I am still going for treatment.'

One of the most remarkable things about Aamir's character is his ability to confront the reality and deal with it. While interviewing him I had realized he needed some help from a psychiatrist. But I was not sure how he would take the suggestion. I was really amazed how confidently he had said he needed medical help.

He asked whether I knew of a psychiatrist. And I had fixed an appointment with Dr Achal Bhagat.

'Please, remember to mention Dr Achal Bhagat in my acknowledgements.' This was the third time he had reminded me.

Aamir did not feel self-conscious about mentioning he was undergoing psychiatric treatment. It was truly amazing. I asked about the treatment.

'You want to know the truth? The younger therapist started to cry when I told her my story!'

We laugh. The fears and problems Aamir has are very real. I wonder how far a doctor can help him deal with the ever present anxiety about his future and the future of his little family and also about the terrifying political trends.

Then I ask about his mother. She had passed away a few days earlier.

Aamir shows me a photograph of his mother sitting on a chair and Alia and Anusha standing next to her. 'This is our last photograph. It was our last Eid together. Doesn't she look happy? On that day, Alia went to get her food from the kitchen. I changed Ammi's diaper, gave her a glass of water to drink and she was sitting on this chair and she looked at me and her eyes had infinite love. She looked contented. And then she took a deep breath and passed away. It was 9 a.m. on 10 October 2015. At least I was with her for the last few years; she saw her daughter-in-law and her granddaughter...'

And Alia, how was she?

Aamir still had a half embarrassed, shy smile whenever there was any mention of his wife. It was then that the expression in his eyes matched the smile on his lips. He said: 'Alia still complains that I do not take her to romantic movies. Now I like movies with serious themes.'

'I am worried about Anusha, my daughter.'

'Why what happened to her?' I asked a little alarmed.

'The political situation is getting worse. Nitish has won but there is a rise in communalism. I have seen the Muzaffarnagar riots in 2013; the burnt church in Dilshad Bagh in 2014. I have seen for myself the attacks on the minorities. By the time my daughter grows up what kind of world will she see?'

'Should we end your book on this sad note?'

'No. I am not entirely free, but I am not in jail. I am fighting against injustice and if more and more of us join the struggles for democracy and secularism we can change society.'

At first his words sound like empty clichés—but when I look at his expression I can see that the words democracy and secularism have a profound meaning for him. They are the hope with which he lives and survives on a daily basis.

Nandita Haksar
New Delhi

APPENDIX I

138 (2007) DELHI LAW TIMES 759 (DB)

DELHI HIGH COURT

R.S. Sodhi & P.K. Bhasin, JJ.

MOHD. AMIR KHAN —Appellant

versus

STATE —Respondent

Criminal Appeal No. 823 of 2003 & Crl. M. 6130 of 2003—Decided on 4.8.2006

Indian Penal Code, 1860 — Sections 302, 307, 436 — Explosive Substances Act—Section 3—Murder, Attempt to Murder, Mischief by Fire, Use of Explosive Substances — Circumstantial Evidence — Appreciation of Evidence — Presence of appellant at spot cannot be doubted but mere presence not sufficient to bring home guilt of accused to charges framed — Nothing on record to suggest crude bomb blast was handiwork of this accused — Circumstances in this case do not form chain of events strong enough to bring home guilt of accused—Presence of appellant at shop prior to explosion of bomb is only fact deposed to and not planting of bomb—If there were other persons also besides appellant occupying table under which explosion took place appellant cannot be singled out of them in absence of any other incriminating evidence and accused of planting bomb there — Reasoning of ASJ under challenge, unsustainable and set aside — Prosecution failed to adduce any evidence to connect accused appellant with charges framed much less prove them — Judgment of conviction set aside.

[Pg. 763-764 (Paras 11 to 14)]

Result : Appeal allowed.

Counselfor the Parties:

For the Appellant : *Mr. Rajesh Mahajan, Advocate.*

For the Respondent : *Mr. Ravinder Chadha, Addl. Public Prosecutor with Mr. Jagdish Prasad, Advocate.*

JUDGMENT

R.S. Sodhi, J.—Criminal Appeal No. 823 of 2003 challenges the judgment of conviction dated 23.4.2003 and order of sentence dated 8.5.2003 passed by the

Additional Sessions Judge, Delhi, convicting and sentencing the appellant under Sections 302/307/436, IPC and Section 3 of the Explosive Substances Act in Sessions case No. 104 of 1998 arising out of FIR No. 631 of 1997, Police Station Karol Bagh, New Delhi.

2. Brief facts of the prosecution case, as have been noted by the Additional Sessions Judge in his judgment under challenge, are as follows:

> "That on 26.10.97, SI Sandeep Gupta along with HC Makkhan Singh and other police officials were on patrolling duty and were present near Hardayal Singh Road and Azmal Khan crossing, when at about 7.00 p.m., he heard the explosion and he went to the spot *i.e.* Roshan Di Kulfi. The S.H.O. and A.C.P. also came to the spot. Several persons had sustained injuries in the explosion and a substantial damage was also caused to the shop. The injured were removed to Dr. Ram Manohar Lohia Hospital and Sir Ganga Ram Hospital for treatment. Kumari Sonia d/o Sh. G.S. Arora, resident of Basant Vihar was declared brought dead by the doctors.
>
> SI Sandeep Gupta collected the MLC of injured persons and returned back to the spot, where he recorded the statement of Sh. Ashok Kumar Soni, owner of the shop Roshan Di Kulfi.
>
> Sh. Ashok Kumar Soni stated in his statement that he is the owner of the said shop and restaurant Roshan Di Kulfi and on 26.10.97 at about 7.00 p.m., he was present at his shop. At that time, there was a big rush of customers, and eatables were served by the staff to the customers. Suddenly an explosion took place and the entire shop was filled with smoke and several persons had sustained injuries.
>
> IO sent Rukka to the Police Station for the registration of the case, on the basis of which, formal FIR was registered. He also inspected the spot and the scene of occurrence was also got photographed by him and prepared the site plan and lifted the material such as iron pieces, *dibba,* etc., *vide* memo and he recorded the statements of the injured persons and of other witnesses and sent the dead body of Kumari Sonia for autopsy.
>
> During the investigation, the recovered explosive material was sent to C.F.S.L. Chandigarh for analysis.
>
> Investigation of this case was transferred to Crime Branch and on 27.2.1998 accused Amir Khan was arrested in case FIR No. 49/98; Police Station Railway Main Delhi and a revolver and 10 live cartridges were recovered from his possession. The accused was interrogated and he made a disclosure statement and during the investigation, it was revealed that this accused had planted bomb at Roshan Di Kulfi in Karol Bagh."

3. Upon completion of investigation, the police filed challan in Court against the appellant and one Mohd. Shakeel who was allegedly making the bomb and had supplied the same to Mohd. Amir Khan. Charges were framed under Sections 302/

307/436, IPC and Section 3 of the Explosive Substances Act against the appellant only while his co-accused was discharged.

4. The substratum of the allegations against the appellant are that on 26.10.1977 he planted a low intensity bomb in Shop No. 2816/18, Beadon Pura known as Roshan Di Kulfi with intent to cause death of persons at random. The bomb exploded causing death of Kumari Sonia as also multiple injuries were received by several persons besides damage to the property. The appellant pleaded not guilty to the charges so framed and, therefore, the case was put up for trial.

5. The prosecution in order to prove their case examined as many as 62 witnesses which included the injured persons. The appellant took a plea in defence which has been summed up by the Trial Court as follows:

> "That in the year 1997, he had gone to Pakistan Embassy situated at Chanakyapuri for obtaining the visa for visiting Pakistan as his sister was married there. There one Gupta Ji met and told him that he works in Intelligence Bureau, Government of India, and took him to a nearby shop and told him that in case he works for the country, the Government would support him financially and would provide him security. He was asked to collect information regarding the Pakistan Navy, their officers, monograms regarding the Pakistan Navy and also to collect certain documents from a person, who would be meeting him at Karachi. On 12.12.1997 he visited Pakistan to meet his sister and fell ill there. Because of intensive patrolling, he could not collect information, which was required to be collected, but he collected the documents from a person in Karachi and returned back to India on 12.2.98. When he reached at Wagah Border by train, he found that passengers were being searched intensively by the Pakistan Police as well as by the Indian Police and he got perplexed and he had thrown those documents, which he had brought from Pakistan and returned back to Delhi on the next day. Thereafter, Gupta Ji met him and showed his inability to collect the information, on which he was threatened by him that he would be involved in false cases. On 20.2.98 when he was passing through Bahadurgarh Road, he was lifted by some persons in a Gypsy vehicle and was taken to the office, where Guptaji, Ravi Shankar ACP, Ins. Rajender Bhatia, Ins. Rakesh Dixit and Ins. Subhash Tandon were present and he was tortured by them and obtained his signatures on blank papers and was falsely implicated in this case.
>
> He has, however, not led any evidence in his defence."

6. The prosecution's case primarily hinges on the evidence of PW 1, Shri Vikas as also his mother PW 56, Smt. Sushma Narula. PW 1, Shri Vikas, in his deposition states that on 26.10.1997 he together with his mother, Smt. Sushma Narula, Shri N.D. Verma as also his wife, Smt. Namita, and daughter, Shivani, went to Karol Bagh for shopping. While at Karol Bagh, this witness along with others went to Roshan Di Kulfi, Ajmal Khan Road. At Roshan Di Kulfi there was a rush for seats which necessitated some waiting period. After some time, a seat fell vacant in the third row on the left side, probably second or third table. The seat had been vacated by the appellant, Mohd. Amir Khan, who had finished having *gol goppas*. The witness identified the accused on account of permanent cut mark on the cheek. The witness deposes that after 4 or 5 minutes of the accused having vacated the seat and while the witness and the party had taken their seats, a blast occurred. This caused injuries to the witness, his mother, Shri N.D. Verma, his wife and daughter. Thereafter the witness goes on to explain the nature of injuries caused by the explosion. He also states that the accused left the table with a bag in his hand.

7. PW 56, Smt. Sushma Narula, states that on 26.10.1997, she along with her son and neighbour had gone to Karol Bagh for shopping and thereafter went to Roshan Di Kulfi. Since there was waiting period, they waited for 5/7 minutes and saw one table which was likely to be vacated. They went towards that table on which two boys were sitting. One of them had a beard and the other had a cut mark on his cheek. On the table being vacated, this witness along with others occupied the same. She states that immediately thereafter an explosion took place beneath the seat whereupon she sustained serious injuries. The witness identified the appellant as the person who had vacated the seat which was later occupied by her. The other so-called injured witnesses do not identify the appellant.

8. It may be noticed here that besides the evidence of these two witnesses, there is no material to connect the accused with the explosion. It was argued by Counsel for the appellant that taking the testimony of the witnesses, at the highest, what stands proved is that the accused was present at Roshan Di Kulfi, was seated on the seat beneath which a blast occurred after he vacated the same, this evidence, in no way, holds the appellant responsible for planting of the explosive substance which detonated subsequently. Suspicion, howsoever strong it may be, does not take place of evidence. He also submitted that the appellant was arrested in case FIR 49/1998 on 27.2.1998 which is much after the explosion at Roshan Di Kulfi and during the long period of his detention in that case he was shown to many persons and his photographs were also published in newspapers and so appellant's refusal to join TIP, for which application was moved on 30.3.98 was justified and in any case in the application names of witnesses to identify him were not disclosed. Nothing incriminating was recovered from the appellant which connects him with the explosion at Roshan Di Kulfi. It is also interesting that the co-accused, Mohd. Shakeel, was discharged in this case. In the absence of any material to connect the accused with the blast at Roshan Di Kulfi, his mere presence would not be sufficient to bring home the guilt.

9. Counsel for the State has very feebly tried to take benefit of the testimony of the junk/scrap dealer, PW 36, Mukesh Nayyer, who states that the appellant had purchased some junk from him about 3¼ years back. This, Counsel submitted, would be sufficient to show that the material for preparing the bomb was collected by the appellant from the junk dealer and thereafter planted at Roshan Di Kulfi to create terror.

10. With the help of Counsel we have meticulously gone through the record of the case. We find that, but for the statements of PW 1 as also PW 56, there is nothing to suggest that the accused appellant herein had either purchased material for making a bomb, made the bomb, or placed the bomb under the seat in Roshan Di Kulfi. This evidence being woefully absent cannot connect the accused to the crime. Evidence of PW 36, the junk dealer, leads us nowhere since there is no evidence brought on record by the prosecution to show that the iron pieces allegedly sold by this witness to the accused were used in making the bomb which had exploded at Roshan Di Kulfi. In fact even the samples of iron pieces seized from the shop of PW 36 and sent to National Physical Laboratory were not even produced in Court and were destroyed in the laboratory itself. Although prosecution had also examined, PWs 10, 11, 28 and 32, to show that the accused had purchased some chemicals used for making bombs from them but none of them supported the prosecution. Other witnesses examined by the prosecution, as noticed already, are either injured persons who do not even claim to have seen the appellant at Roshan Di Kulfi or are policemen who had taken some part or the other in the course of investigation of the incident of explosion and so their evidence is totally irrelevant as far as the involvement of the appellant in the crime is concerned.

11. Presence of the appellant at the spot cannot be doubted but mere presence is not sufficient to bring home the guilt of the accused to the charges framed. There is no doubt also that the explosion took place soon after the accused left the seat. This fact too, is not sufficient to conclusively infer that the accused had planted the bomb and thereafter left. There is evidence on record to show that the accused himself had partaken in eating *gol goppas* which must have taken some time, but there is nothing on record to suggest that the crude bomb blast was the handiwork of this accused. It may be that the accused-appellant himself providentially escaped the consequences of a blast. Suspicion, if at all, no matter how grave, is no substitute for evidence. The circumstances in this case do not form a chain of events strong enough to bring home the guilt of the accused.

12. The Trial Court in its deliberations has held that accused guilty in paragraph 29 of the judgment which reads as follows:

> "The testimonies of PW 1, Sh. Vikas, and PW 56, Smt. Sushma Narula, duly prove that an explosion was caused by a bomb which was planted by the accused Amir Khan, who was present at the shop at the relevant time, consequent of which the aforesaid several persons sustained injuries and Kumari Sonia later expired."

13. With great respect to the Trial Court, analysis of the testimonies of PW 1 and PW 56 does not lead to the conclusion as has been drawn. At the highest, presence of appellant-Amir Khan at the shop prior to the explosion of the bomb is the only fact that has been deposed to and not to planting of the bomb. The Trial Court has also in paragraph 31 noted "the evidence on record, thus duly proves that

it was the accused, who had planted the bomb in the aforesaid shop." Once again, with great respect, we fail to see which is the evidence on record that duly proves the planting of the bomb by the accused-appellant in the shop. If we look at the chief examination of PW 56, she says there were two boys sitting on the table and PW 12, mother of the deceased, had come out with an altogether different version. She deposed that the table, under which explosion took place, was occupied by 4/5 boys before it was occupied by other family (which was PWs 1 and 56 only). PW 12 does not say that the appellant was one of those boys. In any case, if there were other persons also besides the appellant occupying the table under which explosion took place the appellant cannot be singled out of them in the absence of any other incriminating evidence and accused of planting the bomb there.

14. Having given our careful consideration to the material on record and the reasoning of the Additional Sessions Judge, we are of the opinion that the judgment under challenge cannot be sustained. The prosecution has miserably failed to adduce any evidence to connect the accused-appellant with the charges framed much less prove them. Accordingly, the appeal is allowed and the judgment of conviction dated 23.4.2003 and order of sentence dated 8.5.2003 are set aside. The appellant who is in custody, be released forthwith, if not wanted in any other case. The appeal and the application stand disposed of.

Appeal allowed.

Note: As can be clearly seen there are numerous spelling errors in the Court document above. Aamir's name has also been misspelt as Amir. This is the case in many other documents and notices as well.